Christians and the Great Economic Debate

Christians and the Great Economic Debate

J. PHILIP WOGAMAN

SCM PRESS LTD

334 01931 1

First published 1977
by SCM Press Ltd
56 Bloomsbury Street, London

Printed in Great Britain by
Western Printing Services Ltd
Bristol

Elizabeth Bimelle
August 1977

1. Economics and Christianity

Contents

Preface

In some of the Western democratic countries, the term 'great debate' is used to speak of widespread public discussion of momentous issues. In Great Britain, a great debate preceded entry into the Common Market. Americans engaged in a long great debate over civil rights legislation in the 1960s. Great debates often deal with specific policy questions. But they usually call forth consideration of profound philosophical differences and long run consequences of historic magnitude. A great debate may focus upon decision by Parliament or Congress. But its participants include other kinds of opinion leaders and large numbers of ordinary, intellectually alert citizens.

This book is based on the belief that humankind is engaged now in a great debate of worldwide and historic magnitude on the question of how economic life should be organized. Aspects of the debate are peculiar to each country, but it will ultimately be decided in world, not national terms. The broad outlines of the great economic debate call forth a new global consciousness. It is not likely to be resolved quickly.

The last great economic debate occurred in the 1930s, in the midst of worldwide depression and political unrest. It concerned the unhappy coincidence of unemployment with unused factories, idle resources and hungry people. Traditional capitalist economics seemed unable to find adequate solutions to put people and resources and machinery back to work. The great debate included the question of the proper role of government in the economy. It involved national monetary policies and the role of the banks. The debate was largely ideological, with capitalists and socialists and Communists of varying hues participating. Christians of many lands became involved, most notably through the great

Oxford Conference on Life and Work in 1937. The great economic debate of the 1930s was largely resolved along the lines of the 'new economics' set forth by John Maynard Keynes and his followers, except in those countries which came under Marxist domination and those countries yet underdeveloped.

Keynesian economics has dominated policy in the non-socialist countries for more than thirty years. During this time, extremes of laissez faire capitalism and Marxian socialism have clearly been on the defensive. But as the world moved into the 1970s a series of economic problems sent shock waves across Western Europe and North America, with reciprocal effects in other parts of the globe. Some of the problems had natural or political causes – such as severe crop shortages, an overall energy shortage, the Middle Eastern oil embargo, and the swelling pressures from liberation movements in Third World countries. But many people were also ready to conclude that Keynesian economics had finally proved inadequate as an overall approach to political economy. Contrasting ideologies, from left to right, are no longer so much on the defensive. Once again the ideological debate has been joined.

This is most obvious in the electoral politics of the Western democracies. Most of the national campaigns in these countries during the 1970s have been dominated by major unresolved economic issues. For example, the 1976 US presidential campaign between Gerald R. Ford and Jimmy Carter was deeply affected by economic problems and questions – especially by the relationship between unemployment and inflation and by the size and effect of the Federal budget. Economic considerations have similarly affected politics in Great Britain, Australia, West Germany and other countries. This should be a reminder to us that politics and economics affect each other profoundly. It is well to remember, in the discussions of economic ideology in this book, that even laissez faire capitalism is implicitly a political as well as an economic point of view. Other ideological tendencies are much more explicitly political.

Christians are a minority in the world's population, and even among themselves they are deeply divided on ideological questions. Nevertheless, their active participation may serve the great economic debate well. For to the extent that they can do their thinking as Christians, they will help to keep the focus upon the deeper human value questions and to promote the consciousness that what is at stake in economic questions is the well-being and community relationships of the whole human family, each of whose members is a person of incalculable worth.

This book is written as an aid to Christian thinking on these matters. I am painfully aware that I have not recorded the last word on the subject. But if the book contributes to greater clarity in understanding the issues and in comprehending what may be at stake in choosing among the great ideological options, I shall be amply rewarded.

I am grateful to President John L. Knight and the Board of Governors of Wesley Theological Seminary for the study leave during which most of this book was written and to the Association of Theological Seminaries in the United States and Canada (and the Andrew W. Mellon and Arthur Vining Davis Foundations) for a faculty research fellowship which helped to support this period of work. Most of the work was done during a time of residence in Great Britain, and I wish to record my thanks to the Cambridge University Society for Visiting Scholars and to Wesley House and Fitzwilliam College for friendly hospitality in various forms. The libraries of Cambridge University and the London School of Economics and Political Science extended many helpful courtesies. Several economists, including A. B. Cramp, Maurice Dobb, Lord Kahn, Owen Nankivell, and Joan Robinson graciously shared valuable insights with me, as did church social action leaders Giles Ecclestone and Luther Tyson. The manuscript itself was helpfully criticized by Dr Tyson and Professor Larry L. Rasmussen. Of course, none of the above is to be held accountable for errors of fact or interpretation in this book. I wish also to record my gratitude to my secretary, Mrs Carolyn Schneider, for typing the final manuscript and maintaining the flow of transatlantic correspondence relating to it. As always, my wife and children provided innumerable forms of support and encouragement during the period of this work.

Wesley Theological Seminary
Washington, DC

J. Philip Wogaman

To my colleagues

I

Is Economics beyond Morality?

> In a few years all our restless and angry hearts will be quiet in death, but those who come after us will live in the world which our sins have blighted or which our love of right has redeemed. Let us do our thinking on these great questions, not with our eyes fixed on our bank account, but with a wise outlook on the fields of the future and with the consciousness that the spirit of the Eternal is seeking to distil from our lives some essence of righteousness before they pass away.
>
> Walter Rauschenbusch (1907)

This modest proposal by Walter Rauschenbusch has been neglected by most discussions of economic matters. It is not just that people have always had a certain tendency to think first of themselves. The problem is that for at least two hundred years they have been told that it is *wisest* not to make economic decisions directly on the basis of moral considerations.

It is ironic that this advice was first given in intellectually respectable form by a moral philosopher, Adam Smith. In his *An Inquiry into the Nature and Causes of The Wealth of Nations* (1776), Smith advanced the then novel viewpoint that

> Every individual is continually exerting himself to find the most advantageous employment for whatever capital he can command. It is his own advantage, indeed, and not that of society, which he has in view. But the study of his own advantage naturally, or rather necessarily, leads him to prefer that employment which is most advantageous to the society. . . . In this case, as in many other cases, he is led by an invisible hand to promote an end which was no part of his intention. I have never known much good done by those who affected to trade for the public good.[1]

While many people have disagreed with them, those famous words have almost been the moral text for two centuries of economics. For even those who disagreed have tended to think of economics as an autonomous sphere of human life, better not subjected to direct scrutiny in relation to moral values. Sometimes the principled selfishness of Adam Smith has even been echoed by moral leaders, though seldom as blatantly as by the nineteenth-century Bishop William Lawrence who declared that 'Godliness is in league with riches'.

To be sure, part of the difficulty has been a lack of clarity concerning 'morality' and 'ethics'. Many people think of these terms very narrowly. Often morality is thought of simply in terms of private virtues such as honesty and sexual decency, and ethics is seen as a matter of rules concerning right and wrong conduct. Sometimes people have thought of these terms more freely as having to do with love, but love defined quite individualistically. Frequently there has been a tendency to regard morality and ethics as subjective matters which ought not to be permitted to upset the objective workings of economic life.

This book is based on a much broader understanding of morality and ethics. These terms really have to do with our basic values. What do we consider to be 'good', and why do we think of it as *good*? Why is something 'better' than something else? Why does something 'matter'? Seen in this light, all of life is infused with moral questions and problems. Every decision we make, every judgment we render, every action we propose to take – unless it is utterly trivial or wholly technical – has a moral dimension. I will suggest below that it also has a religious dimension if, with H. Richard Niebuhr[2] we think of religion as having to do with the value centre on the basis of which we value everything else. But whether or not that is so, we can scarcely treat economics as autonomous from the moral realm if we believe that anything of value is at stake in economic decisions. Even a decision to subordinate everything else to getting rich is a moral decision, although it is increasingly understood to be a disreputable one. Even Adam Smith's reliance upon the invisible hand is a moral position, as he himself fully realized, although it has tended to insulate economics from direct moral evaluation ever since. Perhaps two hundred years after the publication of *The Wealth of Nations* it is time to remove this insulation by subjecting the economic patterns and philosophies of our time to the most careful moral scrutiny.

The times are ripe for this task. It has, in fact, already begun in the ideological ferment and controversy of a world in revolution. It has also begun in the quiet uncertainties of honest men and women whose lives are remote from the economic battlegrounds but who wonder whether the world's economic life is properly arranged to serve the most basic human needs and values.

The Complexity of Economic Problems

The machinery of economic life can no longer be viewed as morally self-regulating. This means that truly moral judgment has become much more difficult. Economic life is incredibly complex – so much so that we may doubt whether anybody fully understands it. Two or three illustrations may help to make the point.

Consider, for example, the problem of the relationship between inflation and full employment in Western mixed economy systems (economic systems with both a private and a public sector). Economists believed that a major break-through had occurred in our understanding of how to handle the evils of recession and inflation through the Keynesian revolution. In a nutshell, that revolution (named after the British economist Lord Keynes, whose 1936 book, *The General Theory of Employment, Interest and Money* set forth the major points) was a revolution in our understanding of why recessions occur and what government can do to alleviate them. It involved a basic understanding that recessions and depressions occur because there is not enough demand (or purchasing power) for the products of industry. Without demand, industry could not continue to produce and to expand with new investment. Plants would close down, creating further unemployment and lowering the available purchasing power still further. During the Great Depression Keynes and others came to realize that the important thing was to enlarge purchasing power and expand new investment (new investment, it was discovered, has a 'multiplier effect' in expanding the jobs and income of workers). So, by expanded public works and lowering taxes government could stimulate the economy and reverse the vicious circle of recession. It did not matter that the government's budget would run a deficit, partly because a stimulated economy would in time generate greater tax revenues but also because there is nothing intrinsically wrong with public debt.

Where, on the other hand, there is inflation it is because there is too much purchasing power – too many dollars or pounds or francs bidding for the same goods in an economy already producing full tilt. Then the problem is to reduce demand, by increasing taxes or encouraging private saving or some other device.

The main outlines of the theory seemed amply justified by the experience of the Depression, World War II, and later. Though tried on a limited basis during the 1930s, Keynesian economic policies did at least help to arrest further economic decline and to stimulate greater economic activity. But World War II really seemed to make the point, for under the pressures of a wartime situation, governments greatly stimulated production. With full production for military goods and with full employment, personal income was finally sufficient to absorb all the goods and services available in the civilian market. Now the problem was inflation – too much purchasing power. The government handled this mainly through a system of price controls and rationing, combined with patriotic appeals to buy war bonds. Some economists feared a massive post-war return to depression, but the savings of the war years (represented by war bonds, etc.) provided more than enough purchasing power to generate a massive reconversion of the economy to peacetime production with prosperity and minimal unemployment. This and the experience of subsequent years seem to have validated the broad outlines of Keynesian theory.

Nevertheless, beginning in the late 1960s an unanticipated problem began to occur with increasing frequency: the combination of unemployment *and* inflation. Government now faced a dilemma. By increasing purchasing power in order to generate more production and employment, it also seemed to create more inflation: and by restricting the supply of money in order to deal with inflation it also seemed to increase unemployment. This situation, known colloquially among economists as stagflation (stagnation + inflation) is described in the Phillips Curve – a graphic representation of what seems to some economists to be an inescapable correlation between full employment and inflation.[3] The root of the problem apparently is that there are really two kinds of inflation: one which is caused by too much demand ('demand pull') and one which is caused by excessive wage increases ('cost-push'). What will work with one will apparently not work well with the other.

I do not wish to suggest that economists have no ideas in dealing with this problem. But the various conflicting solutions point all too clearly to the fact that there is not yet any really clear understanding of the problem. So how is one to enter moral judgments into such a complex arena?

Another illustration of complexity is the role of the multinational corporations. Much economic literature has been written as if corporate businesses were limited in their primary operations to the countries in which they were based. They might buy and sell on a world market, but their trading partners would be other businesses based in their own countries. It was therefore easier for economists to understand governmental management of a national economy since government had more direct control over business activities within their own national boundaries. In recent years, however, we have seen a rapid increase in the development of multinational corporations – companies with substantial investment and operations in several countries, operating under the regulations of more than one nation.[4] What is the significance of this new development? Nobody is quite sure. Some have hailed this as a new and promising form of internationalism capable of stimulating economic development and growth all over the world. Others are alarmed by it as a new and menacing form of irresponsible power. One book speaks of the multinationals in glowing terms:

> The multinational corporation is the only organization which has resources and scope to think, to plan, and to act with world-wide planning of markets and sources. Many international opportunities require capital and technology on a scale only large multinational corporations can supply.[5]

Another book expresses alarm:

> The global corporation is an instrument for accelerating concentration of wealth. As a global distributor it diverts resources from where they are most needed (poor countries and poor regions of rich countries) to where they are least needed (rich countries and rich regions of poor countries).[6]

Have multinational corporations made an important contribution to the economic development of Brazil and Chile and Iran and the Philippines – or are they mainly the channels by which the resources of such countries are syphoned away to wealthy lands (or something of both)? Can multinational corporations avoid taxes by shifting profits under disguise to their subsidiaries in low-tax countries; do they upset the stability of international monetary exchange by shifting their funds about; do they make it difficult for national governments to control inflation and recession? Or are they really weak sisters, vulnerable to expropriation and oppressive control by irresponsible governments?

These giants are not altogether unknown, of course. But their full economic significance is obviously complex, important, and puzzling.

Even if we fully understood problems of controlling inflation and recession and large business activities, there would still be the problems of resource scarcity and ecological imbalance. Nobody knows, for instance, exactly how much petroleum and coal exist under the earth's surface, but these are clearly limited resources of energy. Some day, perhaps within two or three decades in the case of oil, they are bound to run out. Then what? Can a properly stimulated (capitalist or socialist) economy be counted upon to come up with new inventions and fuel substitutes at the right time to replace the diminishing energy sources? Or, as another complexity, how are we to resolve the dilemma of fuel conservation versus ecological pollution. In order to cut down on pollution we place exhaust emission devices on new automobiles; but these devices lower the mileage per gallon of those automobiles, making us use up the limited supplies of petroleum faster. Raising the price of petroleum helps to limit consumption to the most necessary uses, but this also raises the price of fertilizer in desperately poor countries like Bangladesh.

Of course these complexities only scratch the surface. Economics is not a simple thing, and we may very well be sceptical of those who claim to have all the answers. The facts are never all in. No experts have all of the available facts in their brains, and it is common for experts to disagree. It is not surprising that laypersons are simply overwhelmed by it all.

Coping with Uncertainty

How are we to make moral decisions and judgments in spite of all this uncertainty?

That is not just a problem for us in dealing with economic life. Almost every aspect of human experience is complicated. When we make our decisions morally we can only rarely be *certain* we have done the right thing. Even such 'simple' things as raising children and deciding upon a job leave plenty of room for doubts about the outcome of our decisions. Still, as moral beings we have to make our decisions and live with them. And we had better be able to make them with some self-confidence if we are not to be completely demoralized by them.

One approach to this problem has, in some areas of life, made it possible for people to make decisions with some assurance despite factual uncertainty. That approach is to try to establish where the main presumption should lie, and then require deviations from the presumption to bear the burden of proof. We 'presume' certain things to be good or right or true unless we are given ample reason to believe otherwise. Or, to state this differently, we try to decide what will receive the 'benefit of the doubt' in case there continues to be doubt.

This is the approach used in a criminal court, where the accused person is 'presumed' to be innocent until he is proved, beyond reasonable doubt, to be guilty. This is the approach followed by most executives or administrators who, after all, cannot be expected to have at their command all the factual expertise to arrive at a decision. Such decision-makers tend to seek out information and opinions from the generally acknowledged experts in a particular field, and then to 'presume' the rightness of the information or opinions, unless, after testing the expert, some contrary view is clearly more reasonable. Thus, a medical doctor's opinion will be given the 'presumption' over that of a layman or a quack. This does not mean, of course, that one simply decides in advance of all evidence that every accused person is innocent and that every expert is right. Only a foolish person would fail to examine all the evidence to the best of his or her ability before finally deciding. But if, after examining the evidence carefully, there is still uncertainty, the matter will be decided in accordance with one's initial presumption. One does not, by this method, arrive at certainty. But one does have a way of deciding things with greater assurance.

Later, in Chapter 3, I want to suggest several moral presumptions which, I believe, can serve as a strong basis for judgments having to do with economic life. But for now, several rather simple presumptions which often guide economic policy-making can be mentioned to illustrate the use of presumption in this field. The general presumption of most people in labour-management relations is usually against strikes. All but the most conservative among us support the right of collective bargaining by unions. But we (including most union members and leaders) regard a strike as a weapon of last resort. The burden of proof is against it. It will not be used or approved of unless it seems to have been necessary beyond reasonable doubt (although labour and management will of course disagree as to when, if ever, it is in fact necessary). On the other hand, once a strike has been declared, all union people – whether or not members of the affected union – will have a strong presumption against crossing the picket line. Some make this an absolute, although with most union members it is simply a very strong presumption. One does not cross a picket line unless there are overwhelmingly strong reasons for doing so.

Another illustration: ever since Adam Smith capitalistic economics has usually had a presumption in favour of competition in business. Laws against monopoly were fairly late in coming; but when they did they were an attempt to support what was already a long-standing view that every monopoly enterprise should have to bear the burden of proof. It was assumed that prices would be lower and enterprises would be more efficient if businesses had to compete among themselves for the market. Until forty or fifty years ago this was, in fact, a typical argument used against labour unions, for the latter were considered to be monopolies of a very important commodity – namely, labour. (In the United States legislation was enacted in the 1930s which declared that 'labour is not a commodity'.) In some fields, such as utilities, transportation, and communication, it has become evident that competition often does more harm than good – but this has always had to be established beyond reasonable doubt.

In the United States there has always been a dominant presumption against governmental interference in the economy. When in doubt, according to the presumption, private enterprise should be permitted to do things in its own way. This presumption has been particularly set in the United States against actual public ownership of enterprises, although even here – as in the case of the Tennessee Valley Authority and the postal service – the 'burden of proof' has been met for some kinds of governmental ownership. In the socialist countries, on the other hand, the burden of proof has been against private enterprise. In the Soviet Union, Lenin set out to collectivize the whole of industry only to discover that it would be necessary, at least in the 1920s, to encourage some carefully regulated private enterprises. Some private enterprises and franchises exist throughout the Marxist world today, although these have been permitted only because a doctrinaire refusal to do so would *clearly* damage the forward movement of the economy.

Of course, some of the most interesting decision-making situations occur when presumptions turn out to be contradictory with each other, and then we have to choose which presumption should be given the real benefit of the doubt. The classic case, referred to above, involves the twin presumptions in favour of full employment and against inflation. Both of these presumptions are important in many Western policy-making circles today. But the moment of truth comes when such policy-makers believe that some more unemployment must be created in order to bring the inflation rate down or when some more inflation must be accepted as the price of fuller employment. By and large, policy-makers will take one action hoping it will in the long run cure both the problem of inflation and that of unemployment. But for the short run, it is often believed that a choice must be made.

Other kinds of presumptions could be listed. Some people

have a fairly strong presumption against going into debt and certainly against defaulting on a debt once it has been made. Many people have a presumption in favour of honesty in their business dealings.

I suppose these are not things we think about very much on the conscious level. Yet, if presumptions such as these shape our basic judgments and decisions, then we certainly should try to be as clear as we can about them. At the very least, it will help up to understand ourselves better and, perhaps, to clarify the disagreements among persons who respect one another. Careful examination of our working presumptions in the light of our most basic moral values may even bring us to see that our working presumptions are sometimes a denial of the things we really believe in. And then we may have to change.

The Question of Ideology

It will be noticed that the particular presumptions, which I cited as illustrations above, depend to a considerable extent upon some overall viewpoint or other as to how economic life ought to be organized. Some suggest a 'capitalist', others a 'socialist' general attitude.

Most of our particular presumptions do reflect such a wider orientation. Despite widespread criticism of the term (I shall examine the criticisms in the next chapter), I believe the right word to describe these general viewpoints is ideology. I have in mind something like Julius Gould's definition of ideology as 'a pattern of beliefs and concepts (both factual and normative) which purport to explain complex social phenomena with a view to directing and simplifying sociopolitical choices facing individuals and groups'.[7] An ideology is a complex weaving together of values and beliefs. It is our (often unconscious) picture of what society ought to be like. We may believe that this picture describes society as it once was, and therefore we seek to return to that 'golden age' of the past. We may think it describes society as it is, in which case we will stoutly resist all change. Or we may think of it as a vision of what has never been but may someday be, in which case we shall be 'progressive' or possibly revolutionary. Whether ideology represents a 'false consciousness' or doctrinaire rigidity will be taken up in the next chapter. But here let it be freely admitted that all ideologies contain some element of value judgment – some conception of the good. Hence, while ideology is not the same thing as religion or philosophy, it may depend upon values and beliefs which have religious and philosophical origin.

How, exactly, do ideologies help form our particular judgments and decisions?

Interestingly, an ideology can act as a kind of presumption – locating the burden of proof, determining what receives the benefit of the doubt. To take an illustration that is not strictly economic, many Americans and Western Europeans are ideologically democratic in their political viewpoint. As an ideology, democracy is complex. It has a certain history in the thought of the Enlightenment (particularly Locke and Rousseau) and even in the ancient Stoics. It is committed, one way or another, to the value of each individual person and, at the same time, it encompasses a recognition that human selfishness needs institutional restraint. Hence it regards certain civil rights as fundamental, and it believes that political power should be explicitly responsible to the whole citizenry. All of this involves certain values which can scarcely be proved. But democratic ideology also includes a complex series of interpretations of historical events proving, one way or another, that democratic political institutions work best.

Persons committed to this ideological perspective may not believe that *every* situation on earth should immediately be governed democratically. But they will place the burden of proof against everything that seems to be undemocratic. Freedom of the press may not work out everywhere at the present moment but censorship will have to be proved necessary beyond reasonable doubt. Not every expression of religion is socially constructive, but even the most outlandish forms of religion must be tolerated unless there are overwhelming reasons for not doing so – reasons going beyond whether the majority happens to be persuaded by that religion. In some situations majority rule itself may produce sheer chaos, but only with the greatest reluctance will a true democrat give approval to martial law or authoritarian rule.

This presumption for democratic ideology was put to severe

tests during the period of the 1960s and 1970s when vast numbers of people in Asia, Africa, and Latin America were changing their political status. In some of these situations (would Tanzania and Indonesia be good illustrations?) it proved difficult to establish democratic institutions immediately, and a certain amount of one-party and even one-man authoritarianism seemed to have been necessary to lay the foundations for later development. In the Philippines when the Marcos government suspended the constitution and dissolved the legislative assembly in 1973 this was widely viewed with alarm by democratic people everywhere. Yet some convinced democrats within the country considered this a regrettable necessity in the control of serious internal disorder, political corruption, and economic stagnation. The burden of proof was against it but, for some at least, that burden had unfortunately been met by a bad situation. There seemed to be enough good reasons to set aside the normal presumption in favour of democratic process.

Other kinds of ideological presumption could be mentioned. In most societies, the world over, there is a kind of ideological support for monogamous marriage and family relationships – with certain variations of values and beliefs involved. Those believing in this ideology could be expected to be strongly opposed to divorce, but not necessarily unalterably so. For sufficient reason, the normal presumption might be set aside and a divorce accepted. The laws of most countries are in fact based on exactly this approach, for divorce is permitted but elaborate precautions are provided to make it a last resort. The same ideology creates even stronger presumptions against polygamy, a point on which Western laws are generally quite absolute. But persons believing in this ideology have nevertheless been known to accept the existence of polygamy in other cultures rather than do greater damage by trying to interfere with it.

Ideologies are always complicated and subtle, but they are none the less very real in forming our perceptions of what is at stake in the particular judgments we are called upon to make.

In the great economic debates of our time, I believe we can locate five main ideological tendencies: Marxian Communism, laissez faire capitalism, social market capitalism (the mixed economy), democratic socialism and economic conservationism.

A sixth, traditional feudalism, has had enormous importance in shaping social and economic perceptions, and it still enjoys considerable vitality in isolated places. But it is everywhere on the defensive and, I believe, it is no longer a live option. The five main tendencies, then, will be weighed below, on the basis of moral considerations to be introduced and on the basis of their adequacy in dealing with the real world.

First, however, it is necessary to take seriously the views of those who believe we can and should move beyond ideology to what they consider more realistic and less self-interested approaches to economic life. That will be our task in the next chapter.

2

Can we avoid Ideological Thinking?

> We cannot agree about how ideologies came to be. . . . We do agree that ideologies are nasty things – not something we could ever take seriously, but important because so many of the mob around us take them very seriously.
>
> H. M. Drucker (1974)

That is, perhaps, the majority report of twentieth-century intellectuals on the subject of ideology. Indeed, ever since Napoleon spoke with derision of the French 'ideologues' there has been at least a faint suspicion that sensible people do not think in ideological terms. The fact that people holding this view, for different reasons, have called each other ideologues should not stop us from taking their views seriously. I have asserted in the chapter above that we *have* to think ideologically, and therefore we had better take up the objections to that assertion honestly. What is at stake in the discussion? It is certainly not the word itself, for that has admittedly been used in a variety of ways and would not be indispensable. But as I have used it, the consequence is whether or not we can (as sensible people) organize our thoughts about the economic structures and relationships of life within a value perspective. This is a crucial question, although that also does not warrant our side-stepping the objections to ideological thinking.

One of the most formidable objections to ideological thought has been the judgment that it is pre-scientific. In the economic thought of the last two centuries this has been argued both from the extreme right and the extreme left. On the right, laissez faire capitalism believes it has discovered the laws of motion for permanent progress and prosperity. On the left, Marxism teaches a 'scientific socialism' which exposes the fatal flaws in capitalism and the inevitability of a new socialist order. Each regards the other as, at best, a pre-scientific ideology and itself as free from ideological taint. For our purposes, what is most important is that each considers its position to have been derived from scientific analysis and not to be dependent upon moral value considerations. Neither considers it necessary or desirable to rely substantially upon appeals to the conscience, though both consider themselves to be in accord with rationality.

It will not be possible here to explore all of the nuances of both of these systems of thought, yet the central claims of each should be understood.

Is there a 'Scientific Capitalism'?

Does capitalism exist on a scientific foundation needing no support from moral values? As we have seen, that is the tendency of Adam Smith's thought – even to the point of suggesting that economics will work out best if fueled by out-and-out pursuit of self-interest.

In the twentieth century, such ideas have been put forth in most unadulterated form by neoliberalism. Deriving their name from nineteenth-century laissez faire liberalism (and not, of course, from twentieth-century liberalism which tends to mean exactly the opposite), the neoliberals call for a return to total free enterprise without governmental interference as the only way to maintain sound economic life. As a value system, i.e., as an ideology, the neoliberals' ideas must be weighed in moral as well as factual terms. But what is interesting for now is that the neoliberals do not regard moral appeal as necessary in making their case for laissez faire capitalism. Their views are not unlike those of the Marxists, although their conclusions are radically different.

In one version, Howard E. Kershner writes of 'the inevitable bankruptcy of the socialist state'.[1] According to Kershner, economic prosperity is possible in the long run only with free enterprise in which there is an open market price system and in which each person is paid in accordance with his contribution to society (as determined by the open market). When this kind of system is replaced by socialism, only disaster lies ahead. As Kershner develops the scenario, a socialist government usually comes to power after a long period of capitalist prosperity. The government makes people happy for a time by distributing the wealth accumulated under free enterprise. But, since 'no socialist system has even shown itself to be the equal, or anywhere near the equal, of free enterprise as a producer of wealth', the wealth produced previously is used up. There is less and less capital investment. Production slackens. There are more and more scarcities. The state increases its indebtedness in order to keep on doing more and more things for people. Inflation increases. The state increases its taxation of its productive citizens for the benefit of the less productive class, and eventually it crushes initiative and incentive. It is more and more difficult to keep up production. Finally, the socialist state 'goes deeper and deeper into debt until bankruptcy, usually through inflation, takes place'.

This scenario depends pretty obviously upon Kershner's view that capital formation (the increase in productive capacity) is not possible under socialism – and also upon his view that public debt is a prelude to catastrophe. Both views are thoroughly naive, even though each may contain some element of truth. If anything, socialist countries can be accused of placing too much stress upon capital formation to the detriment of consumer goods. And, since Keynes at least, it has become clear that public debt – far from being an ominous portent of disaster – is necessary for the sake of stability and economic growth. The socialist countries have, indeed, experienced some inflation; but inflation has been less of a problem in those societies than it has in the West. Moreover, the socialist countries have not had the accompanying problem of rising unemployment. Other problems, the socialist countries certainly have had – but not the ones suggested by Kershner.

A more sophisticated view has been advanced by the two dominant writers of the neoliberal persuasion: Friedrich A. von Hayek and Ludwig von Mises. Von Mises is clear in his judgment that laissez faire capitalism is based on science and not upon appeal to moral values: 'Liberalism is derived from the pure sciences of economics and sociology, which make no value judgments within their own spheres and say nothing about what ought to be and about what is good and what is bad, but, on the contrary, only ascertain what is and how it comes to be.'[2] Specifically, liberalism has it on scientific grounds that socialism will not work: 'What liberalism maintains . . . is simply that for the attainment of the ends that men have in mind only the capitalist system is suitable and that every attempt to realize a socialist, interventionist, agrarian socialist, or syndicalist society must necessarily prove unsuccessful.'[3]

According to both von Mises and von Hayek, the thing that socialism cannot do is allocate resources on a rational basis. It is all very well to talk of centralized planning but, according to these neoliberals, the planners will never have enough information in hand to develop their plans. Why not? With division of labour in a complex industrial economy, there are simply too many economic facts for any one person or group of persons to master. Production involves hundreds of thousands of components and decisions and end products and a vast number of specialized labour functions. To co-ordinate all this is simply not possible. The genius of the free market system, on the other hand, is that through the pricing mechanism nobody has to know everything. The laws of supply and demand will in themselves guarantee that resources and finished goods go to the most efficient uses. For instance, if the price of certain raw materials is rising, this means that those raw materials are more needed and, with the rise in prices, it will be more feasible for enterprises to increase the supply. Where prices are falling, the opposite message is transmitted – namely, that the materials are less in demand. These 'signals', while providing the necessary information concerning resource allocation, also indicate where investment will prove feasible. Enterprises which do not observe the signals clearly and produce efficiently will fail, and their productive resources will be taken over by more efficient producers. Thus, under capitalism, while nobody has all the information needed for planning, the system works efficiently and productively. Lacking this kind of information system, socialist leaders 'would not be able to decide which of the innumerable possible modes of procedure is the most rational. The resulting chaos in the economy would culminate quickly and irresistibly in universal impoverishment and a retrogression to the primitive conditions under which our ancestors once lived.'[4]

Von Hayek and von Mises also make certain moral claims for free enterprise, including their view that it alone can sustain political freedom and provide for equitable distribution of goods. But, for now, we must ask ourselves whether they have placed a scientific foundation under their system which needs no further moral argument.

Obviously, history has not been very kind to some of their views, For example, whatever problems there may be in the USSR or China or Eastern Europe, we can hardly describe these as areas of 'universal impoverishment and a retrogression to the primitive conditions under which our ancestors once lived'. Since there has been steady economic growth in the USSR for nearly sixty years, we may also doubt whether that particular scenario will ever come to pass.

But even on theoretical grounds, there is a central flaw in the argument. This was revealed as long ago as the 1930s by the socialist economist Oskar Lange, who demonstrated that a socialist economy could function with the equivalent of a market system.[5] A central planning board could, under socialism, establish prices for all commodities and products. It would know when the prices were too high by the increase in inventories; it would know when the prices were too low by the existence of shortages. Its management of a rational economic plan would in no way require private ownership of the means of production. More recently, the Czech economist Ota Sik and some other socialist economists have called for radical de-centralization of socialist economies, making full use of market pricing and competition, but retaining social ownership of production. Except for Yugoslavia, socialist countries have not opted for this approach; but their reluctance seems more political than economic in origin. Von Hayek and von Mises have, in any case, certainly not demonstrated that a market pricing system would not be possible under socialism. Therefore, the bottom falls out from under their central thesis that a socialist system would *necessarily* prove impracticable.

But the neoliberals have also failed to prove that pure capitalism will itself necessarily work. In their theory, the market system will always function at full employment. Without governmental interference, prices will always find their own level. Workers will always receive enough in wages to provide adequate market for the goods they produce, since all costs and profits eventually find their way into wages and further capital investment. It will always be profitable to make and sell goods because there will always be a market. Neoliberals continue to accept 'Say's law', according to which supply always creates its own demand and everything that is not consumed is bound, through saving, to be invested. But economists now know that 'Say's law' is not necessarily valid. It is possible, as the great depression illustrated, for money to be hoarded and not invested when business concludes that there will not be a sufficient market for their goods. It is possible for an economy to bog down into long term stagnation. The very governmental interference which the neoliberals so greatly despise may have been the only thing that preserved capitalism at all during the depression.

This is not to dispose of capitalism as an ideology, but only to say that capitalism, like socialism, cannot rest its case upon *scientific* grounds. Its various claims and contributions must be weighed and measured in moral and not simply scientific terms.

A 'Scientific Socialism'?

If anything, Marxism has been even more explicit in rejecting any 'ideological' thinking. Its major thinkers have treated economic and social matters as fully scientific and therefore not dependent upon value judgments. The *locus classicus* of Marxian claims for scientific socialism is Friedrich Engels' little book, *Socialism: Utopian and Scientific*. Engels begins by criticizing both the Enlightenment 'kingdom of reason' and the utopian socialists of the century preceeding his own time. While accepting certain elements in each, he dismisses them finally as ungrounded in relation to the real world. The following passage, in which he speaks of the utopian socialists, provides us with the flavour of his views:

> The Utopians' mode of thought has for a long time governed the socialist ideas of the nineteenth century, and still governs some of them. Until very recently all French and English socialists did homage to it. The earlier German communism, including that of

Weitling, was of the same school. To all these socialism is the expression of absolute truth, reason, and justice, and has only to be discovered to conquer all the world by virtue of its own power. And as absolute truth is independent of time, space, and of the historical development of man, it is a mere accident when and where it is discovered. With all this, absolute truth, reason, and justice are different with the founder of each different school. And as each one's special kind of absolute truth, reason, and justice is again conditioned by his subjective understanding, his conditions of existence, the measure of his knowledge, and his intellectual training, there is no other ending possible in this conflict of absolute truths than that they shall be mutually exclusive one of the other.... To make a science of socialism it had first to be placed upon a real basis.[6]

What, then, is that real basis? It is, first of all, founded in the materialistic conception of history. The materialism of which Engels speaks has often been misunderstood. He does not mean that people only act on the basis of materialistic motives or that only material things have any importance (in fact Marxism, as we shall see later, is quite definitely interested in man's spiritual nature). What it does mean is that the form of our institutions and social attitudes is based, finally, upon economic forces: 'the final causes of all social changes and political revolutions are to be sought not in men's brains, not in man's better insight into eternal truth and justice, but in changes in the modes of production and exchange.' Therefore, he added, the causes of social changes 'are to be sought not in the *philosophy*, but in the *economics* of each particular epoch'. When we perceive that social institutions are unjust this 'is only proof that in the modes of production and exchange changes have silently taken place with which the social order, adapted to earlier economic conditions, is no longer in keeping'. The time has come, in other words, when economic changes have made previous social relationships and attitudes obsolete. Social change becomes more or less inevitable, although human actions can speed up or slow down the process.

'Scientific socialism' is specifically based upon the judgment that, under the conditions of modern industrial production, the means of production are in conflict with the patterns of business ownership and direction, or, as Engels puts it, 'the mode of production is in rebellion against the mode of exchange'. The mode of production is social – that is, many people work together co-operatively, with highly specialized tasks allotted to each, in producing the end product. But the mode of exchange is based upon private property and conducting business for a profit. This means that the productive enterprise will function, and *it will only function*, when a profit can be made for the owners.

Does this simply mean, as the capitalist might say, that only efficient and socially useful enterprises will be able to continue in business? Not according to Marxism. For what may be socially useful for the mass of people in the way of production of goods may not be useful for the owners in the way of profit.

The economic analysis used to back this up emphasizes the concept of 'surplus value', which is another term for profit but which carries the judgment that profit is that part of the value created by the labour of workers which is not returned to the workers. The importance of this in economic terms is that 'the expansion of the markets cannot keep pace with the extension of production'. In a word, there is not enough purchasing power out there to buy the products of enterprise, partly because the workers have not been paid enough and partly because of the unevenness of development between those industries producing things for consumers and those devoted to producing machinery with which consumer goods will later be produced. On the basis of this analysis, Marx and Engels developed an interpretation of industrial crisis, the concept of the 'industrial reserve army', and the 'increased misery' theory.

Industrial crisis is the point when there is no longer the possibility of producing for a profit because industry has expanded beyond its market. As recession or depression set in. Weaker firms are the first to lay off employees. Since these workers are without income this further undermines the market, and other enterprises have to discharge workers. A vicious cycle thus sets in, and soon a vast number of people are unemployed. The 'industrial reserve army' is the army of the unemployed. During normal times there are always some unemployed people because this is necessary to keep wages down. During the peak of production there may be something like full employment, but during a recession the reserve army will be very large indeed. The 'increased misery' theory was an earlier Marxist notion that, with each cycle of full production and industrial crisis, the reserve army would enlarge and the economic condition of the workers would become progressively worse. Thus, Marxism believed, the basic contradiction between social production and private ownership could lead to deeper and deeper social crises until finally the whole system would be overthrown and a more rational and humane form of exchange, corresponding to the mode of production, could be established.

Even stated in this rather elementary way, the theory has marks of plausibility about it. Why, after all, *should* there be the periodic spectacle of unemployment when workers were perfectly willing, even eager to find jobs; and why should factories be idle when people were in need of what they could produce?

As a basis for 'scientific' socialism, however, the original Marxian conception ran into difficulties. The industrial crises did continue, to be sure, but the overall condition of the working class seemed to be getting better in the industrial countries, not worse. Nor were the workers in the predicted revolutionary mood. (Even to this day, the only countries in which the socialist revolution has in fact occurred have been those with a primarily agrarian, not industrial economy, or those which were compelled by the Soviet Union to become socialist following World War II.) How could one continue to speak of a 'scientific' socialism in Engels' sense?

Lenin's doctrine of imperialism was destined to play a crucially important role.[7] According to Lenin, the enterprises of the industrialized countries have been able to postpone the final day of reckoning by, so to speak, exporting the problem. Excess capital could be invested abroad in the underdeveloped countries; which is to say, workers who might otherwise be unemployed in the industrial countries are kept busy producing machinery and consumer goods for the underdeveloped regions. And the (largely peasant) workers of those regions are employed at very low wages, extracting raw materials to be shipped back to the industrial country in exchange. The financial mechanisms whereby business capital from industrialized countries is thus employed are detailed. The doctrine of imperialism has accomplished several important things: It has provided a reason why the final collapse of capitalism has been so slow in coming. It explains why the workers of advanced countries are relatively well-off. It explains why the socialist revolutions could occur in the more backward areas first (because the contradictions within capitalism are experienced there most acutely). And, perhaps most importantly so far as Marxism as a revolutionary doctrine is concerned, it provides a theoretical basis for regarding peasants in such areas as workers in the world-wide industrial complex of capitalism – as a part of the proletariat.

But the doctrine of imperialism was developed more than half a century ago. Much has happened in the meantime. The successful revolutions in Russia, China, Cuba, Vietnam, etc. could be taken as proof that 'scientific socialism' really does describe the inevitable course of history. But these events could also be provided with broader interpretations: they are not unambiguous evidences for scientific socialism. (For instance, in a number of cases, including China and Russia, land reform was an important motivation among the masses who made the revolution. But land reform had as its goal the more equitable distribution of private land holdings among the peasants – hardly a *socialist* objective.)

More recent Marxist economists have, accordingly, sought to provide updated interpretations of capitalism. The Cambridge economist Maurice Dobb, while agreeing essentially with Lenin's doctrine of imperialism, suggested that the development of labour unions in the industrial countries has heightened the problem for capitalism. Restriction of imperialistic outlets forces capital to seek renewed investment opportunities at home. But this is more difficult because of the unions which impede the re-development of an industrial reserve army.[8] The basic contradictions remain in capitalism, but now it is more difficult to predict precisely how and where the breakdowns will occur: 'I believe that the right way of looking at economic crises is to regard them, not as the inevitable product of any one particular form (or aspect) in which the essential contradiction of capitalism appears (that between the developing forces of production and profitability for capital), but rather as an expression of this basic contradiction which may manifest itself in a variety of particular forms.'[9] 'It is accordingly possible,' he continues, 'that different booms may break, not for the same, but for different reasons (so far as proximate or immediate causes are concerned); and what this particular reason is can only be discovered by studying the concrete circumstances and sequence of events of the boom in question.'[10] Dobb believed, even prior to World War II, that

> ... it was far from the intention of Marx that his analysis of capitalist society should provide a few simple principles from which the whole future of that society could be mechanically deduced. The essence of his conception was that movement came from the conflict of opposed elements in that society, and from this interaction and movement new elements and new relationships emerged.[11]

The American Marxist economist Paul Sweezy has emphasized the importance of the development of monopoly capitalism.[12] Acknowledging that Marxism has been slow to understand that capitalism is today no longer the primarily competitive economy that Marx experienced, Sweezy has set forth an analysis of class conflict and surplus value in this new context. In this newer situation, the great corporations, such as General Motors and Ford, may compete with one another, but they rarely do so through price-cutting. Prices are set and profits are guaranteed through a system of price leadership in a particular industry. But economic resources are increasingly wasted through large-scale advertising efforts which are of no real social value whatsoever. Continuing industrial production without disastrous industrial crises is made possible only by these increasingly costly advertising efforts and by huge outlays by government for military programmes (the latter also having no social value but being useful to the capitalists in maintaining control of the backward areas where imperialism flourishes). Thus, while out-and-out economic disaster is avoided or at least postponed, workers receive a smaller and smaller proportion of the benefits of their own production and the contradictions within capitalism become increasingly acute. In some of his more recent writings, Sweezy interprets the successful revolutions in Cuba and Vietnam and the increasing unrest within the capitalist countries as evidence of the heightening of these tensions. The basic irrationality of monopoly capitalism will, he believes, continue to become more evident.

Both Dobb and Sweezy – along with most other Marxist writers – combine their economic analyses with expressions of moral outrage. But for present purposes, we need to ask whether scientific socialism is still a live option *as science*. For it to be so regarded in Engels' sense of the term, it must clearly point toward the inevitable collapse of capitalism. To keep the prospect alive on this basis it would seem necessary to demonstrate that a capitalist or mixed-economy capitalist system could not be managed in such a way that waste and crises are avoided.

Western economics may not be in very good shape at the present moment, but *that* point simply has not been made. Concerning imperialism, there probably is a good deal of exploitation going on (an important moral question involving our sense of justice). But the scale of imperialistic relationships between advanced countries (particularly the USA) and the underdeveloped lands is not consistent with the view that those industrialized areas *depend* upon exploitation. Here there may well be distinctions to be drawn among industrialized countries. Great Britain and Japan are seriously dependent upon sources of raw materials; but the United States, the capitalist and supposedly the imperialist giant, is not. The US is a net *exporter* of raw materials. Indeed, with respect to food, until quite recently, the US was basically *giving* food away to less developed countries such as India. The United States has been favoured by the resources of a vast continent. It is not fully self-sufficient in resources, of course. But the resources the US depends upon from abroad, such as bauxite, chromium, rubber, could either be paid for at above fair world market prices or substitutes could be found at home. These points are not intended as a justification for American imperialism or as some kind of neo-isolationism or self-congratulation. Nor is this to say that the American economy does not benefit greatly from exploiting the Third World. The more limited point we are making is that the Marxist doctrine that capitalism *must* break down without imperialistic outlets is not a doctrine than can be proved scientifically.[13]

Does that miss the point the Marxists are making? The real question is, does American *capitalism* have to have such outlets in order to avoid stagnation? Here we must return to the Keynesian problem introduced in the first chapter. Governments clearly can manage economies in such a way that surplus value (which is another name for capital formation) does not, as such, gum up the works. The problem is to keep everybody working, to keep prices reasonably stable, to provide for adequate expansion of industrial capacity, and to maintain market demand. The question of who *owns* the capital does not, in principle, seem crucial either in the short run or the long run in determining whether the economy will work without breaking down. (Although it may be an important question for other kinds of reasons having to do with justice and social responsibility, which are largely moral, not scientific questions.) If one wants to be scientific about it, it may be observed that societies can exist for centuries with gross injustice and exploitation. And, for that matter, economies can be impoverished and stagnant in perpetuity (what educated person could not think of numerous illustrations?).

No, Marxism cannot rest its case on the scientific level. It must take its place among the *ideological* forces contending for the mind and conscience of mankind. Other things will need to be said about it on that level; the force of its claims on that level will have to be taken seriously. We must not be surprised if we find ourselves being influenced by Marxism at many points of specific analysis or judgment, just as a surprising number of fair-thinking people have begun to be. But we are not talking about a Marxism which has replaced ideology.

The well-known Cambridge economist Joan Robinson, herself very much influenced by Marxist economics, has rendered substantially this same verdict on 'scientific socialism'. She writes that 'there is no inherent logical impossibility in conceiving of a capitalist system enjoying continuous expension' and she finds no basis for 'the view that there is an inescapable necessity for capitalism to run down'.[14]

Marxism has not, therefore, provided us with a way of avoiding ideology.

Thus, to summarize, the maximum claims of Marxist scientific socialism were destroyed when it became clear that advanced capitalist countries could regulate the business cycle so as to avoid ruinous degrees of inflation and depression and when it was understood that these countries were not dependent upon colonial empires and imperialistic exportations of capital to maintain economic stability at home. And the maximum claims for a scientific capitalism were destroyed when it was demonstrated that social planning in a socialistic economy is possible without sacrificing the cost-determining mechanisms of the free market. With this undermining of the central myths of, respectively, laissez faire capitalism and Marxian socialism, the problem of economic organization emerges again as a moral question above all. Our organizing perspective, our ideology, cannot be a pure gift of science alone – either capitalist or socialist. We must also be open to moral value considerations.

Pragmatic Objections to Ideology

There is, however, the question whether ideology gets in the way of down-to-earth, practical problem-solving.

The point of view emerged in the late 1950s and early 1960s that mature Western civilization had outgrown ideology. Our new style in approaching problems was not ideological but pragmatic. Daniel Bell's book, *The End of Ideology*, sets the tone. According to Bell, 'in the last decade [the 1950s], we have witnessed an exhaustion of the nineteenth-century ideologies, particularly Marxism, as intellectual systems that could claim *truth* for their views of the world.'[15] While intellectuals, particularly younger ones, still yearn for the all-consuming 'cause', ideology has become 'intellectually devitalized'. 'Few issues can be formulated any more, intellectually, in ideological terms.'[16] This is partly because most issues have become more complex than the ideological frames of reference into which they might be cast. It is also because the dominant concerns of politically decisive segments of the population are for practical goals and not 'causes'.

In economics, this new pragmatism most frequently found its expression in the 'mixed economy' view that it is a mistake to think in terms of pure capitalism or pure socialism. Instead, we should solve economic problems in the best way. Some enterprises, such as the schools and postal services and perhaps even some basic industries, should be socially owned and operated. Others should be left to private enterprise.

Those who continued to take ideology seriously were described as in the title of Eric Hoffer's best-selling book, as 'true believers'. They were understood to have rigid views of life, to be so in need of a cause that they could no longer address life on its own terms. To them, ideological correctness seemed more important than meeting genuine human needs. By contrast, the pragmatist was genuinely alive to the multifaceted variety of the human scene. It could never be said that he or she 'loved humanity but couldn't stand people'.

The pragmatic style probably corresponds closely enough to the dominant view of middle-class people in our time to require no further characterization. But the question must still be raised whether this is a substitute for ideology. Certainly it may be an effective antidote to ideological rigidities, including those of 'scientific socialism' and 'scientific capitalism'.

Still, it must not be forgotten that even the pragmatist addresses life in terms of values, and his or her basic perspective on society is infused with value commitments of various kinds. A problem-solving approach is based upon those values, for what is a 'problem' if it is not a tension between values and reality? To illustrate this point: during the days of civil rights conflict in the American South, racial segregation was a serious 'problem' to most black people and to their white liberal sympathizers. But it was no 'problem' at all to conservative whites who were quite content with things as they were. A 'pragmatist' drawn from the first group would be concerned with concrete ways of overcoming segregation. A 'pragmatist' from the second would be looking for ways of cooling things down and avoiding further controversy. Problem-solving is always based upon one's definition of the problem, which in turn is based upon one's values. Thus, in economic terms, is it a 'problem' that there is vast inequality between the richest one-fifth and the poorest one-fifth in a given society? Is it a 'problem' that unions have the market power to contribute to cost-push inflation? Is it a 'problem' that a relatively small number of people are able to make basic economic decisions for all the rest?

Economic pragmatism may include any of the following ideological components: belief in freedom, concern for maximum production, concern for efficiency in production, concern for protection of the environment, a desire to deal with helpless members of society, and so on. Contrasting and partly overlapping lists of values and objectives could be constructed for capitalist pragmatism and socialist pragmatism, for African or Latin American pragmatism, for British or Spanish pragmatism. And so on.

If pragmatism has a fault it may be in its tendency to take its most basic goals too much for granted (without subjecting them to criticism) and to rely too much upon pure intuition. But, as Louis Wirth remarks, 'The most important thing . . . that we can know about a man is what he takes for granted, and the most elemental and important facts about a society are those that are seldom debated and generally regarded as settled.'[17] These are the ideological questions.

Ideology and Self-Interest

There is, however, a much more searching question to be raised. It is whether our ideologies, even though expressed in terms of high-sounding values and ideals, are only a cloak for our self-interest. The question was raised in a penetrating way by Marxism: ideological thinking is false consciousness; it is based upon our concrete interests. Capitalist ideology, replete with the language of 'freedom' and the 'worth and dignity of each individual' and 'the inalienable rights of man', is finally only a support for vested property interests in capitalist society. Freedom is the freedom to exploit. The 'dignity of the individual' really means the rapacious, rugged individualism of the entrepreneur. Jeffersonian democracy is 'bourgeois democracy', which is simply justification for state protection of bourgeois interests. Every ideology must be examined for its 'taint' – ideological taint is the taint of self-interest which it strives to support but at the same time to conceal.[18]

We may pause to note that there is enough truth in this to make everybody whose ideologies correspond to their privileges a little uncomfortable. How, for example, can a beneficiary of capitalism comfortably go about preaching the virtues of free enterprise in, say, a Latin American favela or among Southeast Asian peasants? Doesn't it seem a little like defending a *status quo* which the American finds quite satisfactory but which the poor people of Latin America or Asia find bitterly unjust?

But 'ideological taint' is a far more pervasive and subtle problem than most of those who speak of it imagine. Self-interest can find support in the widest possible spectrum of ideological views. It has become commonplace even among radical Marxists to view the ideological taint of Soviet apparachiks with disgust; for it is well-known that a class of bureaucrats exists in the USSR which enjoys enormous privileges, even on the crass material level, through the operation of a social system supported by a kind of socialist ideology. But ideological taint is even more subtle than that. Everything that can become a desired possession, including power and prestige as well as material objects, is potentially the basis of self-seeking. Ideological taint is involved whenever ideology supports any such possession whatsoever. Therefore, even radical 'anti-ideological' writers can acquire a vested interest in the success and popularity of their views – at least on the level of prestige, and possibly also on the levels of power and material self-interest. Where such forces are not operative, it is possible that self-interest has taken a more perverted form in the desire for martyrdom and masochism – if there is any truth at all in what psychology has conveyed to us about neurotic forms of self-fulfilment.

Does this mean, then, that all ideology is hopelessly tainted with self-interest? Not at all. It merely means that if 'ideological taint' potentially colours everything, it can, as a ground for objection, exclude nothing in particular. Ideologies, ideological claims and counter-claims need to be examined on their merits. It is not enough to reject or to accept an ideological claim solely because it corresponds to somebody's self-interest. A defensible ideology will indeed correspond to *everybody*'s self-interest, at least in the long run. But in the short run we need to be aware that ideological taint is potentially a factor in every viewpoint.

To be sure, this fact must also affect our judgment of what kinds of ideologies are truly adequate as descriptions of the human condition. But that point will be discussed later.

Joseph Schumpeter's reaction to the Marxian doctrine of ideological taint is a balanced appraisal.

> Social location undoubtedly is a powerful factor in shaping our *minds*. But this does not amount to saying that our minds are exclusively shaped by the economic elements in our class position or that, even so far as this is the case, they are exclusively shaped by a well-defined class or group *interest*. . . . Marx and especially the majority of his followers assumed too readily that statements which displayed ideological influence are ipso facto condemned

thereby. But it cannot be emphasized too strongly that, like individual rationalizations, ideologies are not lies. It must be added that statements of fact that enter into them are not necessarily erroneous. The temptation is great to avail oneself of the opportunity to dispose at one stroke of a whole body of propositions one does not like, by the simple device of calling it an ideology.... But logically it is inadmissible.[19]

Ideology as False God

We need to be aware of one final objection to ideological thinking. This comes from the theologians who contributed so much to a revival of serious Christian thinking during the middle decades of this century – particularly Karl Barth and Joseph Hromadka and those influenced by them.

Their criticism of ideology was an outgrowth of the central themes of their theological insight into the transcendence of God and the radical new freedom which is God's gift in Jesus Christ. At risk of over-simplification, the main points can be summarized as follows: God, if he is truly God, is greater than any human ideas about him. True worship of God always has a transcendent focus, pointing beyond this world. There is room for only one 'absolute' in our worship – God himself. When we absolutize any human institution or practice or custom or law we are involved in idolatry: we are worshipping as God that which is less than God. The essential nature of God is revealed in Jesus Christ, and that nature is one of pure, unbounded love for each of us. In response to that love, we can only love in return. Being faithful to that love involves us in the tasks of this world, including certainly the political and economic power struggles of our time. But we can be faithful in our participation in these struggles only if we are liberated from pre-commitments as to the best possible goals to seek. In every new situation we must seek new insight into the unique direction called for by God's redemptive love.

On the basis of this kind of perspective, Hromadka and his followers in Czechoslovakia were penetrating in their criticisms of the legacy of many centuries of 'Christendom' – the ecclesiastical civilization which conferred extraordinary powers and privileges upon the representatives of the church and which, on every hand, invited people to identify particular aspects of culture as absolutely 'Christian'. This unity of cultural power with Christian symbolism was idolatrous; it led the faithful away from God, not toward him.

Of course, it is easy to see how ideology could fit into this scheme of criticism. Democracy, capitalism, socialism, fascism – do not all the 'isms' smack of this idolatry of human rights? How can we commit ourselves to ideological constructs and remain faithful to the God beyond all these cultural gods?[20] Up until at least the middle 1960s the dominant movements in Protestant Christian theology were sharply critical of ideology; really the mood was strikingly parallel to the pragmatic tendencies of the same period. And after that, when Christian thought as well as secular movements became much more radical, it is questionable whether theologians had quite come to grips with the earlier criticism.

But Christian theology, in the final analysis, could no more dispose of ideological thinking than could pragmatism. What, after all, does it *mean* in concrete earthly terms to speak of God's concern for all his children? It is one thing to seek to avoid idolatry of earthly things. But it is quite another to think of God in entirely other-worldly terms – which the Barths, Hromadkas, Bonhoeffers, Niebuhrs, Tillichs etc., never wanted to do. Such a God would be a denial of the incarnation and would give rise to a false spiritualism undermining belief in God the Father who created his world. That generation of theologians was very active politically and socially, although it tended to proceed intuitively and not often with ideological clarity. But to think of God's concern for this world really means that we are committed, in some form, to the idea that certain solutions to problems are more a reflection of God's unbounded love than are others: and that is also where our biases had better lie.

All this may well have something to say to us about how we do our ideological thinking, and about *what* values are important, and about things that are to be avoided. It may instruct us in the tentativeness with which all human valuation should be held. But this theological perspective cannot excuse us from making ideological choices and forming our judgments ideologically. After all, who among us now would say that racism is anything other than contrary to truth and human good? Should not the contrary of racism, then, form our judgments on racial matters? Do we have much difficulty, broadly speaking, in making a choice between fascism and democracy? Perhaps we shall have greater difficulty in wrestling with the contending options in economic ideology, but this does not make the struggle and the choices any the less important.

Before addressing these options directly, then, we are led to the problem of the source and nature of the values we think important in judging ideological claims. We have seen, in this chapter, that ideology cannot be evaded. The term, by itself, is not a smear word. It is a necessary part of every-day, normal moral thinking. But it still makes all the difference whether our ideologies really do conform, on the one hand, to all we consider good and humane and true and, on the other hand, to the facts of the real world.

3

Moral Foundations

If ordinary people are confused by economic complexities they are no less baffled by the wide range of viewpoints in ethics. What moral values can guide us best in relation to economic matters? Can any of the inherited moral codes help us? Does 'situation ethics' provide any relevant answers? Are any of the older natural law conceptions still useful in the twentieth-century world? Should we look first to religious ethics or to an ethics which all could subscribe to regardless of their religious views?

Not surprisingly, in view of the great diversity of ideas about moral values, some people have concluded that each person's ethics should be a private matter. But even though ethics *is* a private realm, it is also a very public and social one. Every discussion of common objectives breaks down unless it is possible to talk about shared goals and values. There is great diversity in the current landscape of ethics. But that does not mean that we can afford to stop discussing economic matters in moral terms – even if this simply means that we come to understand our disagreements better. After all, even clarity in disagreement can be an important accomplishment; although, as John Courtney Murray once remarked, it is a very rare one.

Economics and Rational Morality

When economists themselves are not simply indulging in moral over-simplifications (such as basing everything on the one value of individual freedom or the one value of production), they have usually sought guidance in rational moral philosophies. The great nineteenth-century debates, for example, were usually fought out in the framework set by utilitarianism – the view that we should be guided by the value of happiness. Happiness seemed to be a universal good, and it seemed possible to think rationally about how happiness could be attained for oneself and for society. It also seemed relevant to economic policy problems via the principle, 'the greatest happiness for the most people'. For the increase in economic well-being of people has always seemed closely related to increase in happiness.

Utilitarianism doubtless has had some significant contributions to make – particularly in the social movements of nineteenth- and early twentieth-century Britain. It has nevertheless proved an uncertain source of ethical guidance for two main reasons. First, it is difficult to reconcile the various conflicting views people have had of what happiness is. John Stuart Mill's attempt to distinguish different qualities of happiness was not very successful. (Mill argued that 'it is better to be a human being dissatisfied than a pig satisfied'. But many pleasure-seekers before and after Mill's time have not agreed.) So how are we to base a universal philosophy on something which people understand in radically different ways? The other problem with the happiness principle is that just because people desire happiness does not mean that happiness is ultimately *good*. Some kinds of alleged happiness certainly do not seem to be good – such as the 'happiness' that sadists take in the sufferings of others. And it is interesting that we often find what we call happiness, not when we seek it directly but when we are pursuing other ends. (A tennis player may feel 'happy' while playing the game, but that is a by-product of the game itself.) So utilitarianism has not proved to be a very satisfactory approach.

A different kind of moral philosophy has recently aroused the interest of economists on both sides of the Atlantic. That is the theory of justice proposed by the Harvard philosopher, John Rawls.[1] Some economists and other students of society believe that Rawls has developed what will prove to be the best possible moral foundation for economic policy discussions. Whether or not that is true, it is clearly a very important one and well worth our attention.

Rawls begins by using an interesting device. He asks us to imagine a situation in which a group of reasonable people had to create a just society from scratch. The one thing the members of the group could not know in advance is what role each of them would actually play in that society. The question then is how they would apportion the responsibilities and the rewards so that each of their own interests would be safe-guarded (without knowing in advance exactly what their own interests might turn out to be). The result of this kind of planning would certainly be objective in the sense that the members of the group would not be thinking of 'justice' in relation to their present vested interests. The emerging conception would not be a simple rationalization for anybody's present privileges. At the same time, the conception would have to be such that each would be benefited regardless of his or her actual future role in society.

According to Rawls, the members of the group, being rational, would decide that the society must be 'fair' to each member. Each must be able to believe that he or she is not being treated unfairly – and so Rawls speaks of the overall conception of 'justice as fairness'. But what does fairness mean? Rawls believes that it means two things most of all: First, it means equality. Everybody must be treated equally or the situation cannot be described as fair. Everybody has to play by the same rules, and those rules can't be 'stacked' in anybody's favour. But secondly, Rawls is aware that absolute social and economic equality may turn out to be to the disadvantage of everybody, including the least privileged members. So what kind of inequality can be accepted? In a society governed by fairness, inequalities can be considered to be just only 'if they result in compensating benefits for everyone, and in particular for the least advantaged members of society'.[2] Inequality cannot be justified by the fact that those who benefit most happen to like it. But it can be accepted if those who are at the bottom of the totem pole feel that they also are better off than they would be in a situation of complete equality: 'there is no injustice in the greater benefits earned by a few provided that the situation of persons not so fortunate is thereby improved.'[3]

From the standpoint of ethics, Rawls' conception is a serious one because it seeks an objective point of reference beyond anybody's particular selfishness. It also provides a potentially measureable starting point (namely, equality) and a method of considering any deviations from that starting point. It fulfils the approach discussed in the first chapter on 'presumption'. The initial presumption being for equality, with deviations required to bear the burden of proof. The burden of proof can be met only when the least advantaged in society benefit from the greater privileges of the most advantaged. Clearly, Rawls believes, every rational person would have to agree with this as the fair and just way to organize society.

We cannot here go into all of the elaborations in Rawls' theory. But those who are not already familiar with his work should bear in mind that Rawls' view is not as individualistic as it might seem on the basis of this short account of it. He is aware that human beings are not merely individuals who are setting about with cold rationality to advance their own interests. The social contract, envisaged by his thought experiment, is not simply a matter of individuals using each other for personal advantage. Rather, in a profound sense it is necessary to our humanity that we find completion through the shared contributions and experiences of the commonwealth: 'It is a feature of human sociability that we are by ourselves but parts of what we might be. . . . The collective activity of society, the many associations and the public life of the largest community that regulates them, sustains our efforts and elicits our contribution.'[4]

I do not wonder that thoughtful economists and policy-makers have been increasingly attracted to the usefulness of this overall theory of justice. I do not believe it is in any important way inconsistent with my own views for, among other things, I shall also wish to emphasize the principle of equality while making room for necessary deviations from it.

But at the same time, I wonder whether Rawls has grounded the conception of justice deeply enough to bear the weight of the hard economic questions. He has attempted to base his theory on a conception of fairness which all reasonable people would accept – thereby achieving a universality of view which might not be obtained if one started from a particular religious viewpoint. But from the standpoint of a moral foundation for economic life something very important has been sacrificed: a grounding in the ultimate *meaning* of economic problems. In point of fact, we do not begin at the hypothetical objective starting point where we are all rational and where we do not have any vested interests to defend. Rawls is perfectly aware of that. But I wonder whether his theory takes sufficiently into account the fact that the well-ordered, just, fair society strikes many people as a game that they have little interest in playing. Until we understand what *ultimately* is at stake in the game – beyond the question whether we feel we are being dealt with fairly in the game ourselves – we may not have a sufficient basis for commitment to it. The point is suggested, rather grimly, by the apparently serious words of a London University economist:

> Suppose that, as a result of using up all the world's resources, human life did come to an end. So what? What is so desirable about an indefinite continuation of the human species, religious convictions apart? It may well be that nearly everybody who is already here on earth would be reluctant to die, and that everybody has an instinctive fear of death. But one must not confuse this with the notion that, in any meaningful sense, generations who are yet unborn can be said to be better off if they are born than if they are not.[5]

Robert Heilbroner who quoted those words commented with disgust that 'thus speaks the voice of rationality'. And he remarks that 'we know very little about how to convince men by recourse to reason and nothing about how to convert them to religion'.

Behind Rawls' idea of justice there is an underlying presumption that human beings are ultimately rational by nature, and that therein lies the meaning of human existence. But such conceptions are religious; they cannot be proved by rational means. If somebody argues that *ultimately* human life does not matter, as Bertrand Russell did in his words 'brief and powerless is man's life; on him and all his race the slow, sure doom falls pitiless and dark', then how can we *prove* the contrary? In an ultimate sense, then, why are we rationally compelled to acknowledge a justice based upon equality when we find other rules of the game more compatible with our current self-interest?

The Theological Contribution

This kind of question is as necessary as it is distasteful to people who really are committed to justice and who are sensitive to humane moral values. Ultimate meaning is finally a question of faith. That point needs to be understood carefully. It does not mean that meaning is just a subjective matter and that all values and viewpoints are equally valid. Nor does it mean that we must abandon rationality. What it does mean is that the nature of the whole of reality is finally beyond rationality. What we believe about the whole is always based upon those aspects of reality which we consider to be decisive as clues to meaning of the rest. This is not a matter of religious thinking retreating step by step before the advances of science, attempting all the while to provide elbow room in the remaining areas of ignorance. The problem is deeper than that. It is plainly inconceivable that human beings should ever have the whole of reality in their brains. Even what we do have is based upon our faith that the perceptions in our heads correspond to real things in the world out there. And who could possibly perceive *everything*, even on this relatively tiny planet. I do not want to belabour the point; but it certainly needs to register with us if we hope to find the truth about ourselves and our moral values.

But everybody does have working ideas about the nature of the whole of reality. For some, the decisive clues are taken from the methods and insights of particular sciences. For them, the world of nature itself provides the decisive clues since this is the world with which science deals. For others, particular personal experiences are decisive, though perhaps not recognized. Some people, who have suffered one reverse after another, may think of reality in pessimistic terms. Some who are overwhelmed by the selfishness and greed of those around them may interpret reality cynically and adapt their moral views accordingly. Many people adopt, more or less, the dominant conceptions of their inherited religious traditions, although these are rarely as simple as they appear on the surface.

I have said that these central conceptions, while being beyond rationality, are not necessarily opposed to reason. One's religious viewpoint may be corrected rationally by further experience, by the findings of science, and so on. One may seek to implement those religious values rationally. One may seek to develop both values and beliefs rationally so that they are mutually consistent and capable of organizing the whole of one's life experience. For example, one may seek to organize economic life in harmony with one's basic religious conceptions.

Does a theological approach to ethical matters mean that it can only be of value to those who accept a particular faith tradition? By no means. One theological contribution may help suggest ways of applying other, very different religious traditions to social and economic problems. More than that, there are important points of consensus among basic faith traditions and philosophical perspectives which can be drawn on only when we approach ethics with theological depth and then share the results. At the very least, we can in this way clarify points of difference. Such differences exist, of course, even within faith traditions. Sometimes there are greater differences of opinion among the adherents of the same faith tradition than there are between some within the tradition and persons who are not identified with it at all.

A Christian Perspective

What then do Christians, as such, have to contribute to the great economic debate?

Their basic perspective is always in some sense dependent upon their belief that Jesus Christ is the decisive clue as to the ultimate nature of reality. In some sense they are always telling the world that when a person fully understands Christ he will not be misled about the final meaning of other aspects of experience. By itself, this may seem less than useful as a contribution to economic issues. But theological reflections on the meaning of Christ have given birth to insights which are profoundly relevant to the important economic problems of the age.

That point is becoming clear in a good bit of the emerging literature of Christian ethicists and theologians on political and economic matters. If anybody believes that Christian teachings are mostly used to sanction an unjust *status quo*, he or she should consult the writings of Third World theologians – and then take note of how their major themes are finding a resonance in the writings of increasing numbers of European and American Christian writers.[5] The day of the simple and simple-minded 'Protestant ethic', with its notion that hard work, thrift, and generosity are a sufficient summary of Christian economic ethics, is now past. Many of the newer writers – one thinks of Gutierrez, Cone, Segundo, Reuther, Moltmann – have in fact been powerfully influenced by Marxism, yet without losing their basic commitment to Christian faith. In their hands, the basic traditional Christian teaching that all human history points toward God's ultimate victory is given great contemporary relevance. Human history, while it will always to some extent resist God's intentions as revealed in Christ, is nevertheless the sphere in which the decisive battles are fought. In Christ we have revealed the new humanity, liberated from the bonds of objective as well as subjective oppression. Freed himself from the social and cultural oppression of all previous history, Christ is the liberator of all who find in him the key to the meaning of life. Nor is this simply an inner 'spiritual' matter. It is that, to be sure; but it is also the strongest kind of affirmation of the demand for liberation in the actual relationships and institutions of human society. Not surprisingly, the exodus tradition from the Old Testament is taken as a powerful preliminary symbol of the liberating role of Jesus Christ. The themes of liberation theology are being elaborated in various ways by different theologians, but all accept liberation and history as decisive elements in relating Christian faith to our time.

This movement will have increasing impact, and I believe it has much to teach us. The theme of liberation is particularly suggestive and, as we shall see, laden with possibilities for an economic ethic. We shall return to this theme later. In the main, however, I believe that the emphases of liberation theology on historical event and liberation *from* oppression do not provide a sufficient overall framework for understanding economic matters in Christian perspective. The striking, even dramatic emphasis upon the movement of history and the struggle for liberation can distract us from careful analysis of ultimate norms. Christian faith concerns our relationships to God, to people, and to the material world. It is these relationships which determine what is at stake when we seek to use the gospel as a source of liberation in the ongoing stream of history. If I may put this in more philosophical language, our metaphysical and ontological commitments are what give ultimate direction to our judgment and actions in the life of the world. These are the commitments that help us determine whether 'liberation' or any other kind of action really matters.

What Christian insight is there, then, into the most basic human relationships? At some risk of oversimplification, Christian faith as a whole can be described as a firm conviction of the goodness of ultimate reality. It is the conviction, nurtured by the quality of the life and self-giving death of Jesus, that God – who is the source of all being – is good and that he cares for each of us with boundless love. St Paul used the symbol of 'grace' in describing this love of God – a word drawn from jurisprudence. While we are all infected by self-seeking sinfulness, God's 'grace' is freely given to us just as, by 'grace', the accused in a Roman court might be released despite his guilt. The crucifixion of Jesus made a particularly strong impression on Paul. Here at the same time were illustrated both the depths to which human sin could descend in the cynical murder of this good man and the limitlessness of the continuing love of that man who thought himself and was accepted by his followers as a channel of God's own love for all human beings in every time and place. In the interpretation of the crucifixion drama, Paul underscores both the boundless love of God and the pervasiveness of human sin. But the love of God is what makes it possible for us to find redemption from our own self-centredness.

The effect of this upon our relationship with others is clear. We can no longer think of other people as alien beings, to be used or feared. We now must think of everybody as a part of the family of God – for his love is equally and freely given to all. As the epistle to the Ephesians puts it, in Christ the 'dividing wall of hostility' which formerly separated us from God and from one another has now been destroyed. In Christ, those who once were 'far off' have now been brought near – and not by right observance of religious practices, either, but by faith in God's love manifested in Christ.

Sometimes the ethical import of Christian faith is summarized in the one word 'love', and that is not a bad or misleading word to use. Nevertheless, the Christian theological perspective requires us to cross the threshold into a new understanding of what the word means. Love, to the Christian, is not simply a matter of sentiment, of emotional feelings. Nor is it just a matter of individuals relating to or doing things for other individuals. As Harold DeWolf and Joseph Haroutunian and others have shown,[6] it involves the whole way we look at other people. Love, to the Christian, is the recognition of the indissoluble kinship we have with others by virtue of our unity in God. Humanity is one family. The recognition of this is what Christian love, at its foundation, means. Man's inhumanity to man is thus always a family question. War is fratricide. Oppression is the dehumanizing relationship of brother and sister against brother and sister. Exploitation is a brother or sister treating another brother or sister as a mere object, a mere convenience. This is true both in the face-to-face relationship and in the mass, impersonal relationship of one great collectivity to another.

As if this were not enough, it is also clear from this that there is a primal equality among human beings which is more important than every form of inequality. The involvement of the church with medieval civilization, with its hierarchical, paternalistic social patterns, has led many to conclude that Christian faith is not so much a commitment to equality as it is the very root of inequality in Western life. But it should be remembered that even in the medieval society – which was surely not egalitarian – a powerful witness to the moral claim of our equality before God was nurtured by the church. When the words 'he has put down the mighty from their thrones, and exalted those of low degree', from the *Magnificat* of Mary, were read out at midnight mass in the medieval cathedral, the shouts of the peasants showed that they understood well enough indeed what those words meant. And were they not echoed by the Chilean peasants whose slogan, however unsophisticated, was 'Marx y Cristo'?

The truth is that the question of equality versus inequality is not settled by what people can do relative to each other, or how high their IQs are relative to each other, or how attractive they are, or any of the various accidents of birth and life. The crucial question is, *what value do they possess*? Are any people *better* or *worse* than others? The answer will be judgment about their relative value. Doubtless some people are more useful than others in respect to certain social objectives. And there is no question that most people value some people more highly than others. But the Christian judgment on this subject of the relative value of human beings is that all are valued equally by God because there is no limit to the value he places upon each and every one. So whatever justifications we may find for policies of unequal treatment in economics, they can never be predicated upon the idea that some people are ultimately better than others. The immense implications of this for economic life will have to detain us later.

But note that these themes, important though they doubtless are on some spiritual plane, can be stated in a kind of material vacuum. Surely if this is a true reading of the heart of Christian faith it has much to say to us about our attitudes toward God and each other spiritually. We ought to respond to God with grateful love, and equally we ought to consider and relate to others as loving brothers and sisters. But this does not yet quite touch the root of the economic problem, for economics has to do with the production and distribution of material and quasi-material things. What does the Christian's spiritual vision have to do with the physical world and the life processes determined by our relationships to nature?

Again, there has often been a kind of suspicion that Christian faith is other-worldly, and that materialistic concerns detract from spiritual ones. That suspicion has been nurtured by the loving words of Christians who exploited one another ruthlessly as if material questions had nothing to do with love. That problem was addressed as early as New Testament times by James, who wrote

> What does it profit, my brethren, if a man says he has faith but has not works? Can his faith save him? If a brother or sister is ill-clad and in lack of daily food, and one of you says to them, 'Go in peace, be warmed and filled', without giving them the things needed for the body, what does it profit? So faith by itself, if it has no works, is dead (James 2. 14–17).

But this rhetoric, pointed though it is, does not yet tell us quite what is at stake in the material realm. The New Testament letter addressed to the Colossians has a magnificent passage on the subject. The passage refers to Christ as 'the image of the invisible God, the first-born of all creation; for in him all *things* were created, in heaven and on *earth*, *visible* and invisible, whether thrones or dominions or principalities or authorities – all *things* were created through him and for him. He is before all *things*, and in him all *things* hold together' (Col. 1.15–17, emphasis mine). In order to understand the obscure language we should remember that it was a response to people who taught that the material world is alien to God. It was an affirmation that the God who is father of Jesus Christ was also the creator of the material world. Hence it is utterly false to relegate God to some 'spiritual' realm as though he had nothing to do with the material one. Notice then the earthy language, combined with a very high conception of Christ as the prime source of our revelation concerning the nature of God.

A Christian doctrine of creation, which this is all about, really is an attempt to understand the relationship between the world God created and the purposes for which he created it. If we understand the basic purposes as involving the loving relationships revealed in Christ, then we have at least a broad notion of why and how the material world is important. It is not important for its own sake, but for the sake of the spiritual realities it helps to serve. In explaining this, I want to avoid the impression of dualism. And yet there really is a kind of dualism implied. Not the dualism of material as evil and spirit as good, but the dualism of nature as instrument and spirit as meaning. Even this can lead to misunderstanding if we think of nature as instrument in the sense of the pillaging of nature for the sake of narrow economic ends. But nature is the whole material realm which provides substance and foundation for the life of spirit. It gives spirit something to work with when interacting with fellow spirit. It gives God a vast, complex channel through which to communicate to humanity, and humanity a rich ground for creative expression.

The point may be better understood if we ask ourselves whether it is better to think of Christian theology from the standpoint of relationships (to God, fellowman, nature) or from the standpoint of eschatology (the movement of history toward God's fulfilment in and beyond time). It is believed by some who prefer the eschatological approach that the relational theme is too passive. A relationship simply exists; as a concept it does not suggest movement. That point is well taken. But spiritual relationship is in no sense passive. It is active, outgoing, expressive; it is giving as well as receiving, celebrating as well as understanding the contributions of others and of God. Spiritual relationship is the interacting of *spirits*. It is too bad that the word 'spiritual', if it does not suggest occult occurrences, sometimes conjures up images of dull prayer meetings and uninteresting people. For the Christian understanding is exactly the contrary. Spirit is life and relationship of spirits is lively interaction. It is endlessly creative. A Christian understanding of relationships and a Christian conception of eschatology belong together.

I have said that the material realm provides the foundation for the life of the spirit. We do not have any idea what spiritual life would be without a material context of some kind. Even the New Testament speaks somewhat paradoxically of a 'spiritual body' after the resurrection of the dead – and the word 'body' seems to suggest that spirit without form is beyond our comprehension. Our physical bodies make it possible for us to experience one another and the whole complex realm of the material. The body is our creative instrument, and nature is the realm of our creativity. Nature is also the realm of God's creative activity, and viewed with the eyes of faith all of our creativity is a response to his.

But just as the body and other material elements provide a channel for spiritual relationship and expression, they can also impede or destroy altogether the life of spirit. Since we are in the flesh, the flesh can be both a means of expression and a means of oppressive control. Taken as a whole, the material realm represents the condition of our existence. Where conditions are not sufficient, the life of the spirit is frustrated. It is true, to be sure, that Christian thought has always acknowledged the heroic victory of spirit over adverse circumstances and the final victory over death itself as a gift of God. None the less, Christian teaching has also emphasized the importance of the quite ordinary necessities of life. The New Testament narratives of the life of Jesus emphasize his role in healing the sick and even in feeding the hungry. The parable of the last judgment in Matthew makes the decisive criterion of moral judgment the question whether one has fed the hungry, given drink to the thirsty, clothed the naked, and dealt hospitably with strangers and the sick and imprisoned. The reason is not just that these are friendly gestures but that without adequate care for the conditions of life we cannot be what God intended us to be spiritually. The occasional triumph of spirit over adversity always presupposes enough of the conditions of existence to make this possible. Have we not learned enough in our time about the dehumanizing of people in death camps and in conditions of extreme poverty to know that for most it is mockery to speak of the triumph of spirit? Sometimes, in such grim settings, there might be a beautiful example of self-giving love, powerful enough to arrest the attention of those spiritually enmeshed in the bitterness of their plight. But the vast inhumanities of Auschwitz and Buchenwald, of My Lai and the Gulag Archipelago, of Bangladesh and the Sahel, tend more generally to overwhelm the spirit. At all events, such gross tragedies illustrate the principle: physical well-being is very important to the health of spiritual relationship.

Is this materialism? If we mean by that word the attitude which treats material things as the goal and meaning of life, then the answer surely is that this is *not* materialism. Nevertheless, while material things are not what life is all about, it is important to recognize that they are necessary conditions to what human life ultimately means. Karl Barth's little formula expresses what I think the Christian perspective must be. He speaks of 'creation as the external basis of the covenant' and of 'the covenant as the internal basis of creation.'[7] Translated, this means that the material realm (creation) represents the preconditions necessary for the fulfilment of the spiritual ends of human life (the covenant). But the spiritual ends supply the meaning of the physical. Material questions can have crucial importance, not because material things are what count but because they are necessary conditions for the things that really do matter. If, as a result of physical deprivation, I die – that is surely the end of me so far as any further spiritual interaction on this earth is concerned. Short of death, I may suffer so much that my full contribution cannot be made and the possibilities within the human family are to that extent never realized.

And so, if we want to know the significance of material things, we must think first of the basic purposes of human life. If we are Christian we will think of God's grace, his redemptive gift of love to every person, his purposes as loving father of the whole human family, and of our possibilities for fulfilment within that family. And then we will think realistically about the material environment which either aids or impedes those basic purposes. The creation or protection of those material conditions is what is at stake, ultimately.

What does Liberation Mean?

Earlier I took note of the viewpoint of 'Liberation Theology' and questioned its adequacy as an overall framework for Christian thinking. I wish now to say that the concept of liberation may have quite useful contributions to make if it is seen in relation to what we have just been saying about human fulfilment in this material world.

In the first place, liberation is a useful concept when applied to human oppression. We can speak of being freed from enslaving relationships of whatever kind. We can contemplate the transformation or destruction of human institutions that enslave the spirit, and of the creation of new institutions that help undergird our true humanity. In the second place, liberation is a useful concept when applied to our relationship to nature. Here we can speak of the liberation from physical deprivation – freedom from want, as one of Roosevelt's 'four freedoms' put it. Liberation can mean freedom from malnutrition, from disease, from ignorance and insularity, even from drudgery. Both kinds of liberation are important. Ultimately they both have to do with the life of the spirit.

In a previous writing, I had occasion to distinguish between 'relative' and 'absolute' definitions of poverty.[8] Absolute poverty was taken to mean the kind of material deprivation which causes real physical suffering or death and which makes it objectively difficult for human beings to find fulfilment. Relative poverty, on the other hand, was deprivation standing in the way of relationships. One could conceive of relative without absolute poverty, and of absolute without relative poverty – although the two often go together. Relative poverty means that one does not have sufficient physical resources to participate as an accepted member of the community. Hence, while many poor people in a wealthy country such as the United States may seem well off compared with the poor of the underdeveloped lands, they are still lacking in the resources needed to function as members of an American community. Their relative poverty is thus real poverty in spiritual terms, and it must be taken quite seriously. On the other hand, it is conceivable that everybody in a given society might be suffering from poverty, but since all suffer together their mutual relationships within the community may not be impaired.

That distinction is applicable to the question of liberation. For liberation can be seen both in that community-relationship sense and in that sense of relationship to the material realm. Both are important. But economic life has played a trick on us; sometimes it forces us to choose between liberation from the oppressions of human inequality and exploitation, on the one hand, and liberation from physical constraints and deprivations, on the other. In our discussions of economic ideology we shall have to be particularly sensitive to how well the various ideologies cope with this important trade-off and, indeed, whether they acknowledge its existence.

The Problem of Human Selfishness

Most of what we have written is, so to speak, on the positive side of Christian faith. It has stressed the positive gifts of God's love, the positive fulfilment in human community, our equality within that community of love, and the positive contributions of nature. An adequate summary of Christian teachings that are relevant to economic questions could not, however, leave out the negative reality of sin. As Reinhold Niebuhr and certain other twentieth-century Christian theologians have shown, there is a profound truth in the traditional doctrine of original sin. (One wag put it that this is the only one of the main Christian doctrines that can be proved *factually*.) The truth is distorted if we think of original sin as being our sexual nature or if we think of original sin in some literal sense as something that stuck to humanity after Adam and Eve first sinned at a particular time and place. The truth can be understood if we reflect on the reality of human rebellion against the good. Why is our attitude so often set against the higher visions of loving community which are represented in in Christian and other religious and philosophical traditions? Niebuhr's penetrating analysis of this question suggests that apart from transforming faith in the reality and power of a source of salvation beyond ourselves, we are driven to seek our own fulfilment selfishly. We are self-centred when we cannot find our true fulfilment in some centre of reality beyond ourselves. When we cannot worship God or some reality beyond ourselves, then we are driven to self-worship.

The truth of this insight into human nature does not depend upon extreme versions of total human depravity. Even the most self-centred Scrooge is doubtless capable of some loving altruism. At the same time, it may be a mistake to think that any one of us is beyond all selfishness. St Paul's theology, referred to earlier, stressed that *all* have sinned and fallen short of the glory revealed in Jesus Christ. Nobody has any reason to boast, for all are in need of God's grace to escape from the trap of human self-centredness. Jesus himself evidently reserved his most scathing rebukes, not for the acknowledged sinner but for self-righteous, supposedly religious people. When we believe ourselves to be completely free of selfishness we may actually be most profoundly sinful in the Christian sense.

This is a dangerous truth. The danger is that we can become deeply pessimistic about human nature and take a cynical attitude toward all human efforts to serve noble ends. We can conclude with Thomas Hobbes that human life is 'solitary, poor, nasty, brutish, and short'. And we can govern our affairs accordingly, which may simply mean that we allow selfishness to reign supreme in our social institutions and practices and look out for ourselves first of all.

But whatever the importance of the reality and universality of sin, the Christian's positive affirmation is of the power of God's love in overcoming that reality. It is a mistake to suppose that any human institution could perfectly represent that love, since sin continues to infect the whole human enterprise. It is equally a mistake to think that human institutions cannot represent that love to greater or lesser degrees. In his discussion of the institutions of democracy, Niebuhr expressed this tension rather well with his famous aphorism: 'man's capacity for justice makes democracy possible, but man's inclination to injustice makes democracy necessary.' Creative social institutions of all kinds represent a positive expression of love, on the one hand, and an effort to guard against the effects of human self-centredness on the other. The really hard questions in economics and other spheres of life often cluster around the degree to which we can place our confidence in love as a dominant human motive and the degree to which we must protect ourselves from the effects of sinfulness.

Such questions are particularly acute when we are dealing with repositories of social power. How can power be used affirmatively to undergird human good without at the same time providing a vehicle for corrupt self-seeking? Perhaps no general answer can be given other than to repeat that it is a mistake either to take sin too seriously or not seriously enough. There may also be wisdom in the idea expressed in the World Council of Churches' conception of the 'responsible society'. That idea is that all who hold political authority or economic power should be responsible to God and to the people whose welfare is affected by it. Where power is meaningfully responsible to the community there is at least the possibility that self-seeking will be kept in check and that everybody will have some sense of participation in the uses of power. Such a call for responsibility in power structures does not in itself settle the ideological quarrels of our time – both laissez faire capitalism and Marxism would claim to fulfil such a requirement – but it may help us to take the reality of sin seriously, though not too seriously, in our further thinking.

Christian Criteria for Economic Ideology

The foregoing can hardly be classed as a fully-rounded explanation of Christian faith! Nevertheless, it may have provided us with the critical points of reference to guide our examination of the major competing economic ideologies of our time. By way of summary, I wish now to suggest the main questions the Christian should ask of every economic ideology. These questions suggest what the Christian may consider to be the most important value presumptions. Where the presumptions are apparently violated in ideological thinking or in economic practice, the burden of proof must be placed against those persons or groups which violate them to demonstrate reasons why it is necessary for the sake of greater human good.

1. *Does the ideology take material well-being itself seriously as a basis for human fulfilment?* We have seen that the Christian perspective on physical nature sees this as God's creation, the sphere for divine and human creativity and relationship. We have seen that maladjustments in the relationship between persons and nature can undermine all that we mean by humane values.

It is implicit that progress in human technical mastery of nature and in production of material goods is in itself to be sought, although it is also implicit that much that goes under the name of progress and productivity is contrary to divine intentions and human good. Wasteful depletion of natural resources and harmful contamination of the environment are against true material productivity. At the same time, improvements in medical technology, transportation, communication, agriculture, and recreational facilities may be highly supportive of human good as the Christian understands it.

2. *Is it committed to the basic unity of the human family and does its view of economic life measure economic success in terms of the economic undergirding of mutual love in the life of community?* To the Christian, the unity of the human community has its source in the creation of all human life by God and in his uniting love. Every divisive practice undermines the true human interest of all, for none of us can find our own fulfilment while remaining estranged from or indifferent to our brothers and sisters.

3. *Does it include belief in the value of each individual human being and is it committed to individual freedom and opportunity for individual creative development and expression?* Concern for individual fulfilment also has its source, for the Christian, in the boundless love of God. That love is not simply social, it is also quite personal and individual. Indeed, it is an important Christian insight that we must never treat the social and individual aspects of human life as mutually exclusive. Ultimately, in fact, we cannot have one without having the other. The value of the individual cannot be sustained apart from his social existence, and society is a meaningless abstraction unless it is made up of individual human beings who are respected as persons. The latter is impossible without a serious commitment to freedom and without the fullest possible opportunity being given for the individual development of talents and abilities and without provision for each to make a creative contribution to the life of the whole.

4. *Does it consider human beings to be equal in a sense that is more basic than any inequalities, and does this guide the formulation of economic objectives and policies?* The equality of human beings has its source, as we have seen, in the equally bound-

less love which God has for all. In that which is most basic, which is in the value of each life, we are all equal. While equality is never a simple matter to understand, much less to translate into actual policies, it may make a great deal of difference whether we acknowledge this as an ultimate claim upon all policy. At the least, equality must constitute a presumption, and apparent inequalities must be required to bear the burden of proof. Otherwise we can hardly be said to take the worth of every individual very seriously.

5. *Does it take the universality of human sinfulness seriously and does it make realistic provision for the effects of self-centredness in its proposed policies?* This question has an important bearing upon our attitude toward social power and the protections we consider necessary to guard against selfish uses of power. But there is also the implied viewpoint that we should avoid ultimate judgments concerning what people do and do not 'deserve'. Christians are warned throughout the New Testament to be especially wary of all self-righteousness. The attitude that we 'deserve' more than others often suggests a degree of self-centredness that is utterly inconsistent with Christian commitment to God and our fellows in the human family.

This is enough for now. These questions may lead us into other issues as we probe the conflicting claims of the dominant economic ideologies of our time, and that examination may in fact reveal the meaning of these points more clearly than this chapter has done. But this will serve to open our insight into what it means to think about things from a Christian standpoint.

Significant Ideological Options

In the chapters that follow, we shall examine five major ideological tendencies of our age. On what basis have the five been selected? The choices may seem a bit arbitrary, and the ways in which these ideologies are formulated may occasionally seem to do only rough justice to the great diversity of viewpoint within ideological schools of thought. This is inevitable. To think at all about these matters we have to simplify, to overlook some things in order to concentrate on what seem to be the most important points. This is what sociologists call thinking about 'ideal types'. None of the following ideologies exists in the pure form they will be characterized in here. Yet the main elements in each of these ideological 'types' have great power in the minds and hearts of vast numbers of men and women in the world today, and it is not possible to get at them without simplification and interpretation.

The five main ideological tendencies I have chosen to explore are Marxism, laissez faire capitalism, social market or mixed economy capitalism, democratic socialism, and what I will call economic conservationism. They will be discussed in that order, although there is no particularly logical reason why.

One final word before we begin this task. We must not begin with the assumption that any one of the five will be completely adequate and that the others will be utterly false. All five of these ideologies originated in Western civilization, and each of the five will be found to share some value commitments with the others. Moreover, each exists in the same world, and consequently the picture of economic realities which each conveys may be similar at points with that of the others. I believe, in fact, that each of these five will be found to have made enduring contributions to economic ethics and that each has some potential blind spots, although this does not mean that the five will prove equally useful to us as vehicles for Christian thinking on economic questions.

4

The Case for Marxism

> If modern Marxism gives the wrong answers, at least it asks the right questions.
>
> Denys Munby (1956)

A modern Marxist might be a bit annoyed by the first half of Professor Munby's statement. But, bearing in mind that Munby is a prominent Christian economist, he might rather appreciate the second part. Since its emergence one hundred and thirty years ago, Marxism has been taken with increasing seriousness as a potent force and an ominous threat. But few people have been able to confront Marxism on an intellectual level and weigh its claims pro and con.

We have already had a brief look at Marxism in order to consider – and reject – its claim to be *the* science of society. But Marxism is more than this claim. It is, in fact, a total creed. It functions in practically every respect as a religion. (John C. Bennett remarks correctly that Marxism attempts to provide authoritative answers to more questions than does Christianity.) This means that when we confront Marxism as an economic ideology we must always be aware of the relationship, in Marxism, between economic questions and other aspects of its overall interpretation of human life.

Before we plunge into this task, we need to remind ourselves of two very important facts. One is that there are numerous schools of thought within Marxism. If Christianity has many denominations and varieties of theological interpretation, so does Marxism. The analogy is really not a bad one. Marxist thinkers range from Joseph Stalin to Erich Fromm; its movements range from Bolshevism to parts of the 'New Left'. A whole vocabulary has developed within Marxism to supply the epithets with which heresies can be condemned: 'revisionist', 'left deviationist', 'Blanquist', etc. Of course there have been increasing numbers of people who have been influenced by Marxism in one or another of its forms without wishing to describe themselves as Marxists. All this means that in constructing the case for and against Marxism as an economic ideology, we shall have to interpret things broadly, and not every Marxist or anti-Marxist will be satisfied with the result.

The other point to remember is that Marxism, as an economic ideology, is not to be equated with the practices of any particular socialist or Communist society. That point is obvious, but it is easy to forget. Several years ago, when the Cold War dominated the thinking of more people than it does today, I recall reading a number of books and pamphlets on Communism versus capitalism, or Communism versus democracy which had been written for high school civics classes in the US and similar mass-education programmes. After a while, I began to notice a typical pattern: capitalist or democratic (often these were equated) *ideals* were being compared with Communist *practice*. That isn't quite fair! It would be like comparing the ideals of the classless society with the 'Christian' *practice* of burning witches or the 'democratic *practice* of Watergate corruption. In evaluating any ideology we have to be aware, both of its theory and of the practical 'track record' of those who have attempted to organize things on its basis. But theory and ideals and practice are not the same thing. When we compare and contrast different ideologies we need to be particularly careful not to compare apples with oranges.

Basic Marxist Doctrine

We have already taken a look at the Marxist conception of 'scientific socialism' and found it wanting. That conception, which emphasizes the ideas of surplus value and the contradictions between private ownership and social production, may contain important insights. But it is not enough to put economic policy beyond the moral debate. Economic history cannot be *counted upon* to work its way out in the direction indicated by Marxist analysis. The further question whether we ought to join the Marxists in the struggle to make it take that direction is a moral question. To get at this question, we must confront the claims made by Marxism at a deeper philosophical level.

The broad outlines of Marxist philosophy are fairly well known. It conceives of all previous history as a series of epochs, distinguished from one another by the forces of production (technology) and relations of production (forms of ownership, distribution, and exchange). In every epoch (with the possible exception of the very earliest tribal societies), society has been divided into exploiting and exploited classes. Thus, in the feudal society of medieval Europe, the two classes of primary importance were the aristocracy and the peasants. The aristocracy governed the peasants, provided them with protection, and in exchange for permitting the peasants to farm the lands, took a substantial portion of each year's crops. The latter was exploitation in the sense that the aristocracy received this 'surplus value' from the peasants without themselves producing anything. In time, the elaborate fixed structures of medieval society became a serious obstruction to the emergence of commercial trade and manufacture. A new class, the bourgeoisie (literally town-dwellers) came into being to develop trade and manufacture and the new epoch of capitalism was soon born. The ideology of the bourgeoisie emphasized freedom above all else – for its major battle was to secure liberation from the constraints of feudalism. In political terms, the battle for freedom was expressed in the democratic revolutions of England, America, and France; in religious terms, the battle for freedom involved the Protestant Reformation. But Bourgeois freedom was not freedom for all, since the bourgeois could not even exist as a class without also bringing a new subject class, the proletariat, into existence.

In his essay on 'The Secret of Primitive Accumulation',[1] Marx argues that there could never have been a capitalism without this new form of class antagonism. What the bourgeoisie call 'capital' is not some abstraction, nor is it simply the accumulated resources of thrifty people. Before there can be such a thing as capital, 'two very different kinds of commodity possessors must come face to face and into contact: on the one hand, the owners of money, means of production, means of subsistence, who are eager to increase the sum of values they possess, by buying other people's labour power; on the other hand, free labourers, the sellers of labour.' In other words, to put this in modern idiom, General Motors cannot produce automobiles just because it possesses factories. There must also be workers available to sell their labour for money wages. So part of the 'liberation' of capitalism was liberating peasants from their bondage to the land and to the aristocrats so that they could become wage workers in mines and factories. Thus, again under capitalism, two antagonistic classes confront each other. As we have already seen in Chapter 2, Marx believed that this confrontation would ultimately contain the seeds of its own destruction. The basic incompatibility between the new social form of production (what could be more 'social' than production for General Motors) and a private form of ownership would in time give rise to revolution by the proletariat. But this revolution would be different from all previous revolutions in that the basic interest of the proletariat is not to create a new form of class domination but rather to bring all class conflict to an end. The new revolution would, in time, usher in a classless society.

Marx and Engels expressed these ideas in an inverted form of Hegelian dialectic: thesis in conflict with antithesis giving rise to synthesis. The nuances of that are hardly worth elaborate exposition since the Marxist analysis does not ultimately depend upon any rigid adherence to this dialectical form – provided we understand that social change occurs through class conflict and revolution. And provided we understand that the root of class conflict is exploitation – expressed in the epoch of capitalism by the appropriation of the surplus value created by the proletariat by the exploiting bourgeoisie. We should also remember that Marx and Engels, despite the moral fervour with which they denounced the evils of capitalistic exploitation, considered the capitalist epoch absolutely necessary in the evolution of economic production. Their *Communist Manifesto*, in fact, is quite lyrical in its praise for the accomplishments of capitalism:

> The bourgeoisie, during its rule of scarce one hundred years, has created more massive and more colossal productive forces than have all preceding generations together. Subjection of nature's forces to man, machinery, application of chemistry to industry and agriculture, steam navigation, railways, electric telegraphs,

> clearing of whole continents for cultivation, canalization of rivers, whole populations conjured out of the ground – what earlier century had even a presentiment that such productive forces slumbered in the lap of social labour.

But having played this role so well, capitalism is now an impediment to further human progress. Marxism's basic analysis would be equally powerful among people who never heard of the Hegelian dialectic, and it is not particularly undermined by an honest recognition of the accomplishments of capitalism either.

What, then, is the heart of Marxism's *moral* appeal?

Clearly it has something to do with the problem of exploitation. The term is constantly employed throughout Marxist literature, but the great revival of interest in recent years in the writings of the 'early Marx', particularly in the *Economic and Philosophical Manuscripts* of 1844[2] has helped to illuminate the meaning of exploitation in all Marxist literature. In those writings, which show considerable reliance upon the German philosophers Hegel and Feuerbach, Marx develops a conception of human nature and alienation. The essence of human nature is to be creative and social. Man is self-creating. By our creative efforts, we actualize what had been only potential before. Put differently, through our work we exercise our human powers, and only in the exercise of those powers are we fully human.

Exploitation, when the fruits of our labour are taken from us, is understood to be a robbery, not just of these material objects themselves but of our life essence. When man the creator is separated from the thing he has created, he is alienated from his own life process. 'Alienation is apparent not only in the fact that *my* means of life belong to *someone else*, but that everything is *something different* from itself, that my activity is *something else*, and finally (and this is also the case for the capitalist) that *an inhuman power* rules over everything.'[3] That inhuman power consists of the abstraction to which all human work is turned: the abstraction of money and relationships of exchange.

We must bear with the fact that Marx's early writings are highly abstract, and that the language depends upon Hegelian ways of thinking that are no longer generally current. The point itself can be illustrated more simply. It is easy to think of an artist finding human fulfilment through a painting or sculpture. The *process* of painting or carving is, in the case of the artist, a fundamental life process. The artist is in the process of becoming more fully human in and through this work of creation. But if the end product, the painting or sculpture, is taken over by others as *their* work then, in a profound sense, the artist's life process has become 'alienated' from him or her. (This may be even easier to illustrate in relation to a political 'ghost-writer' who consciously does his work in full knowledge that his or her boss will receive all the credit.) What does it mean when we say that we have 'prostituted' ourselves? This means that we feel that something in the integrity of our creative process of fulfilment has been alienated from us for the sake of some lesser reward. A prostitute is herself the main illustration of this. Sexual intercourse, which is a creative, loving form of life process, has been sold for money. Its true end, which is fulfilment in loving relationship (and sometimes actual human reproduction) is alienated. The prostitute goes through the motions, not for the sake of that true end, but for the sake of money or some other reward having no inherent relationship to the act at all.

The meaning of alienation may become clearer when its social dimension is understood. Exploitation is a social relationship between one person who has created and another who takes the thing created for himself or herself. Exploitation is when one person 'uses' another. In this kind of relationship, it is impossible for the two to be related to one another as fellow human beings. The exploiter looks upon the exploited as a mere tool. The exploited looks upon the exploiter as an inhuman force controlling his or her destiny and robbing him or her of basic humanity. One of the true ends of all human life process, the binding together of person to fellow person in creative community, has been frustrated. It is an important Marxist insight that everybody involved in this relationship is victimized and dehumanized by it. The exploiter, quite as much as the exploited, is alienated. The exploiter, also, is no longer fully human.

Marx saw this whole process of alienation as particularly endemic to modern capitalism. The wage worker no longer works for the sake of the creative process and its end product. Instead, his or her work is the price that must be paid for the wages to be received. The capitalist uses the worker and appropriates to himself or herself a substantial proportion of the end product of the worker's labour. The two are alienated from such other, just as the worker is alienated from his or her own creative life process. Marx would find the boredom typical of modern industrial workers a striking confirmation. People are not bored when they are doing things they consider to be creative. Nor is this just a matter of dull, repetitious tasks. Every creative person must endure drudgery (we remember Edison's remark that genius is 99% perspiration and only 1% inspiration). But if the goal of the drudgery is *our own goal* then our attitude is likely to be quite different. Make-work projects illustrate the point particularly well; but most wage labour in the modern industrial society does also.

And so the battle to overcome capitalism and to replace it by a classless society in which everyone's contributions are authentically their own without exploitation, is for the Marxist much more than a matter of economic efficiency. Put in such terms, the Marxist would surely be prepared to sacrifice a good deal of productivity and economic well-being in order to straighten out the alienated relationships of modern capitalist society (although the Marxist is also convinced that that society is ultimately self-destructive in purely economic terms as well). This is why criticisms of Marxism based purely upon economic considerations so often miss the point. And this is also why the Marxist has a devotion to this ideology going far beyond what one would expect from an economic conception that is merely considered to be more rational than the others. What is considered to be at stake is our very humanity itself.

This is also the foundation for a Marxist understanding of the sources of anti-social behaviour. People do not act destructively in human society unless they have been frustrated at more fundamental levels. Perverse forms of behaviour – robbing, murdering, lying, sexual assault, embezzlement – are the response to alienation. What the theologian calls sin is here considered to be the reflection of dehumanization, which has its source *sine qua non* in exploitation in a society with class conflict. Thus the abolition of such exploitation is also the basis *sine qua non* for the rooting out of all anti-social behaviour. Marx made this point himself in an article written for the New York *Daily Tribune* on capital punishment.[4] 'Is there not a necessity', he asked, 'for deeply reflecting upon an alteration of the system that breeds these crimes, instead of glorifying the hangman who executes a lot of criminals to make room only for the supply of new ones?'

The perceptive reader will note that more is at stake here even than this. If the causes of crime can be abolished by overcoming the economic basis of class antagonism, then the need for the whole apparatus of the state will also disappear in so far as that apparatus is maintained to keep people in line. That is in fact also an important ingredient in Marxist ideology. It is believed that the successful establishment of the classless society will, in time, also entail the 'withering away of the state'. Marxism has not generally taught that all government would cease. Presumably tasks of administration would continue to be necessary. Some administrative task might even be enlarged. But if we think of the state as embodying the *coercive* powers of society, then that will surely become unnecessary in a society having no need to coerce anybody. The state, even in 'democratic' form, is in reality only the coercive representative of the governing class. A democratic state may be well-disguised, but it finally exists to serve the interests of those who control the productive forces of the society. Whatever its form, the state of the bourgeois society is the governing committee of the bourgeois class. After the abolition of class exploitation, there may be need for the proletariat to exercise coercive power for an interval before the classless society can be fully realized (although this 'dictatorship of the proletariat' has been emphasized much more by twentieth-century Marxists than it ever was by Marx or Engels themselves).

We may note, finally, that Marxist ideology also provides an explanation of religion. It is well-known, of course, that Marxism teaches that religion is the 'opiate of the people'. The term is in no case really intended as a compliment, but it is widely misunderstood all the same. Marxism has been convinced that religion is basically false consciousness. Religion provides an other-worldly interpretation of human relationships which can only be understood concretely in this world. Religion is '*the fantastic realization* of the human essence because the *human essence* has no true reality. The struggle against religion is therefore mediately the fight against *the other world*, of which religion is the spiritual *aroma*.' ('Fantastic' here means in the form of a fantasy.) But in the past epochs of exploitation, the fantasy has still performed a useful function: it has kept alive certain glimmerings of a lost human reality. As an 'opium' it has made the heartless lot of the oppressed more bearable. The classical passage is worth quoting:

> *Religious* distress is at the same time the *expression* of real distress and the *protest* against real distress. Religion is the sigh of the oppressed creature, the heart of a heartless world, just as it is the spirit of an unspiritual situation. It is the *opium* of the people.
>
> The abolition of religion as the *illusory* happiness of the people is required for their *real* happiness. The demand to give up the illusions about its condition is the *demand to give up a condition which needs illusions*. The criticism of religion is therefore *in embryo the criticism of the vale of woe*, the *halo* of which is religion.[5]

So, while rejecting religion ultimately as false consciousness, Marx taught that it once performed a useful role. But – and this is worthy of particular emphasis – the abolition of religion is not taken to be the abolition of man's spiritual life. Quite the contrary. It is the liberated spirit that is alone finally capable of dispensing with the false consciousness of religion. Thus, we have also come full circle in understanding how it is that in Marxist ideology the overcoming of economic exploitation is not only an economic event, but also a spiritual one.

Toward the Moral Assessment of Marxism

Perhaps enough has been said, even in this brief summary of Marxist ideas, to suggest that Marxism can neither be accepted outright nor demolished in one stroke. Christians will recognize here certain themes of enduring significance along with points that seem diametrically opposed to their own peculiar insights into life.

The Marxist doctrine of religion, which is on the face of it a direct challenge to any theological commitments, can actually be by-passed rather quickly. It is not really of the essence of Marxism. That is suggested by the fact that there are Christians today who espouse Marxism in every respect other than in its denial of religion. But it is also suggested by a closer analysis of all of the rest of the Marxist ideological package. The whole concept of alienation, the doctrine of exploitation, the analysis of class conflict, the doctrine of the state, and the other strictly economic themes are all logically consistent with the idea of God. Like the other economic ideologies we are about to examine, the development of the ideology can be considered with or without belief in God. Belief in God is important to the Christian's whole conception of human society and social justice – as we have argued in Chapter 3. But having noted that Marxism lacks this key theological element we can go on to examine the extent to which the other leading ideas in Marxism are consistent with points the Christian (who does believe in God) would want to emphasize.

The theory of alienation is a useful point of departure in this. This is a side of Marxism that Christians must grapple with, partly because it has roots deep in their own faith tradition and partly because this comes close to the point of deep human hurt which has found in Marxism a powerful, though possibly distorted, vehicle. This is a point that the Christian economist Denys Munby seems to have recognized, although he does not attempt to respond to the deeper meanings of the doctrine of alienation:

> The emergence of Communism as a world force threatening the values we cherish is not merely the result of the plotting of a few evil men; it is the inevitable offshoot of a materialistic world, in which the poor were despised, the peasants neglected, the workers exploited, and the victims of the colonial powers uncared for. It is not for those, who have been satisfied with a world in which power and riches have ruled, to object when those they have oppressed proceed to use power and riches against them.[6]

As a world force, Marxism can speak to the conscience of Christians like Munby precisely because it expresses some basic human values which are very close to Christian ones.

In particular we must note the contrast between the Marxist conception of the social nature of humankind and the predatory individualism that has characterized much of Western culture since the emergence of the industrial revolution. The 'principled selfishness' of an Adam Smith – and his numerous followers – has had cultural as well as economic importance. Those who have been taught that things work out best in economics when each person seeks first his own advantage are likely to carry the lesson over into other relationships. They are likely to forget that in a profound sense we all belong to one another in God. The Marxist tradition does not talk about God (at least not positively), but it does have a conception of the human family. Its vision of a restored humanity, in which each person contributes his or her best and is recognized and accepted for that creative contribution, is surely also a very Christian conception. Moreover, its understanding of the damage that can be caused by exploitation, both to the exploited and to the oppressor as well, is a theme with deep biblical rootage. Does one need to cite chapter and verse among the great prophets of the Old Testament and in the sayings of Jesus in the New Testament?

The point is, when we contemplate the Marxist doctrine of alienation we can also come close to an understanding of what is at stake, from a Christian perspective, in economic life. In both Marxist doctrine and Christian tradition, creative labour is fulfilling – both individually and in social nature. And in both traditions it is well understood that we can become alienated from our brothers and sisters and from our 'life process' (as the Marxist puts it, somewhat cumbersomely).

Moreover, despite all the typical misunderstandings of Marxist 'materialism', the Christian cannot find anything to quarrel with directly concerning the Marxist idea of the human spirit. The Marxist does not, we repeat, consider humanity to be *nothing but* material substance; nor does he consider us to be 'determined' in any mechanical sense by material forces beyond our recognition and control. After all, does not Marx himself say that human beings create themselves? When due allowances have been made for the Christian objection that it is God who gives us the capacity to do this, we can find this Marxist idea a strong affirmation of moral freedom.

Still, we are then compelled to turn to a troubling problem. How, if human beings are truly free, can we refer all human sinfulness and evil to structural social problems? Note the awesome importance of that question in the ideological conflicts of our time. *If* human alienation has its source *only* in structural problems of exploitation in a class society, *then* the overcoming of those problems will finally rid us of human selfishness, sinfulness, and evil *forever.* Why forever? Because once the sources of class conflict have been destroyed, nobody would *ever* be motivated to exploit or harm a fellow human being again. If we can truly believe this to be so, then that belief would go a long way toward justifying almost any actions designed to bring on the revolution and, with it, the final destruction of the shackles of human oppression. But if we cannot believe this, then that may have much to say to us about the need to make *continuing* provision for the sinfulness in human life both in the methods we use to seek social change and in the institutions we project for the future of society. It is almost impossible to overstate the importance of this watershed issue in ideological thinking.

We return to the question. How can we reconcile human freedom with the view that *only* structures of oppression cause human sin? On the basis of an analysis of present and previous society, it may not be possible to answer this on an open-and-shut basis. Since there has always been some human oppression, however caused, it is possible to say that every bit of alienated, self-centred human behaviour has that as its source. On the other hand, since there has always been some alienated, self-centred human behaviour, it is equally possible to say that the structures of oppression have *that* as *their* source! But if we are to affirm moral freedom in any ultimate sense, we must acknowledge the possibility that people will sometimes prefer the illusory short-cuts to human fulfilment by seeking to dominate and oppress their brothers and sisters. Moral freedom means freedom to turn away from the good as well as freedom to embrace it. I do not believe a Christian has any business emphasizing this too much, but neither dare he or she ignore it altogether.

The root of the Marxist problem here may be what is in fact an ambiguous relationship between the 'material' side of its philosophy and the human or spiritual side. Marxist materialism is not determinism in the personal or psychological sense. Yet if one is to have ultimate confidence that material relationships are finally decisive, then that carries with it certain overtones of determinism.

But the political problem is more important than a purely abstract discussion of freedom of the will versus determinism. From a Christian standpoint, the most important objections to Marxist ideology may lie with the conception of the state and revolution.

A Christian could readily concede that there is a considerable parcel of truth in the Marxist view of the state as governing committee of the ruling class, at least in the tautological sense that the most powerful elements in any society are bound to have greatest influence over its political institutions. And the Christian, unless he or she is a pacifist, will not dismiss out of hand the possibility that violent revolution could – in an extreme case – be the morally preferable line of action.

At the same time, there are disturbing possibilities in the way in which Marxists generally express their views on the state and revolution. The danger is that we may have here a plausible rationalization for tyranny coupled with a blind spot concerning the wisdom and goodness of revolutionary and post-revolutionary leadership. Any legal safeguards in current bourgeois democratic societies can be dismissed as mere window-dressing for the real power relationships. The need for effective legal safeguards in a future socialist society can be viewed as unnecessary since, in such a society, the objective basis for oppression will no longer exist. In particular, the toleration of opposition parties would be undesirable since any opposition would merely constitute a counter-revolutionary attempt to restore the power of the bourgeoisie. Thus Sweezy writes that '... any particular state is the child of the class or classes in society which benefit from the particular set of property relations which it is the state's obligation to enforce.... If the disadvantaged classes were in possession of state power, they would attempt to use it to establish a social order more favorable to their own interests, while a sharing of state power among the various classes would merely shift the locale of conflict to the state itself.'[7]

Even the Marxist philosopher Herbert Marcuse, who is by no means an apologist for any kind of Stalinism, speaks in this vein. In a discussion of whether social change should be sought by democratic means, Marcuse seems to suggest that real change cannot come about in that way. The passage is worth quoting at some length since it reflects the attitude of large numbers of Marxists around the world.

> The alternative is, not democratic evolution versus radical action, but rationalization of the *status quo* versus change. As long as a

> social system reproduces by indoctrination and integration, a self-perpetuating conservative majority, the majority reproduces the system itself – open to changes within, but not beyond, its institutional framework. Consequently, the struggle for changes beyond the system becomes, by virtue of its own dynamic, undemocratic in the terms of the system, and counterviolence is from the beginning inherent in this dynamic. . . .
>
> But who has the right to set himself up as judge of an established society, who other than the legally constituted agencies or agents, and the majority of the people? Other than these, it could only be a self-appointed elite, or leaders who would arrogate to themselves such judgment. Indeed, if the alternative were between democracy and dictatorship (no matter how 'benevolent'), the answer would be noncontroversial: democracy is preferable. However, *this democracy does not exist*, and the government is factually exercised by a network of pressure groups and 'machines', vested interests represented by and working on and through the democratic institutions. These are not derived from a sovereign people. The representation is representative of the will shaped by the ruling minorities. Consequently, if the alternative is rule by an elite, it would only mean replacement of the present ruling elite by another; and if this other should be the dreaded intellectual elite, it may not be less qualified and less threatening than the prevailing one. True, such government, initially, would not have the endorsement of the majority 'inherited' from the previous government – but once the chain of the past governments is broken, the majority would be in a state of flux, and, released from the past management, free to judge the new government in terms of the common interest.[8]

Eliminated from this analysis, altogether, is the possibility that the governments of the Western democracies are consciously supported by popular majorities or that, if they are, the thinking of these majorities could be changed by anything short of the seizure of power by a revolutionary elite.

Marcuse goes on, however, to acknowledge another potential difficulty: that after the revolution the people will *not* support the new government as an expression of the new common interest. This has, he acknowledges, indeed 'never been the course of a revolution'. But 'never before has a revolution occurred which had at its disposal the present achievements of productivity and technical progress.' Still, he acknowledges that even these technological resources could become only the basis for further repressive controls. In the final analysis, then, he rests his hopes for the future 'on the proposition that the revolution would be liberating only if it were carried by the non-repressive forces stirring in the existing society'. This proposition 'is no more – and no less – than a hope'; but clearly Marcuse does not feel that even the frustration of this hope could lead to a future any more intolerable than the present.[9]

It is particularly interesting that Marcuse can also speak of 'the repressive Stalinist development of socialism, which made socialism not exactly an attractive alternative to capitalism'.[10] But he finds more grounds for hope in the Cuban revolution, Vietnam, and the cultural revolution in China. Perhaps the truly liberating possibilities of socialism can come to fruition in such situations.

We may hope so. But even in those countries power is still exercised essentially by an elite. Perhaps they exercise that power with the sole objective of the interests of the masses – but what ruler has not claimed to do that? We should not quarrel over the good or bad intentions of the present rulers of Marxist countries, however. The real question is whether we should ever trust anybody with unquestioned power. We do not have to agree with Lord Acton's judgment that 'absolute power tends to corrupt absolutely' to see the point that absolute power gives too much opportunity to corruption. The massive evils of Stalinism, acknowledged now by both the friends and foes of socialism, indicate clearly where absolute power can lead. It may not be possible to find in this a final proof that we will always have sin to contend with as a part of the human condition. But we may now say that the Marxist vision of the perfectability of human nature does not confront the full truth about the roots of human sinfulness. Even in a socialist society we should want to have guaranteed civil rights and full political accountability. For despite the selfless devotion to good of many socialists, even that form of society can harbour selfish and power-hungry leadership.

May I make a more modest point? There is a *paternalism* in the typical Marxist political view which also runs against the grain of a Christian understanding of the dignity of all human life. Even in China (perhaps especially in China), where striking claims have been made about the emergence of a new humanity, one is impressed by how the people of the community are patiently led by their more enlightened revolutionary leadership to the abandonment of superstition and wrong ways of thinking. It is quite possible that this elite has been right about most questions and the majority of the people in need of leadership. But leadership without formal accountability surely does create the barriers dividing superior from inferior which undermine self-respect and genuine moral unity. A Christian view of human nature is open to the possibility that every human has something unique to contribute, just as it is aware that no human being has all the answers.

Still, Western Christians must respond with more than defensiveness to a Marxist analysis of their own country's democratic political institutions. That analysis emphasizes that power ultimately is in the hands of the dominant class. As Sweezy puts it, 'votes are the nominal source of political power, and money is the real source: the system, in other words, is democratic in form and plutocratic in content.'[11] Sweezy's own evidence for this is less than overwhelming: political activities, he argues, 'can be carried out only by means of money, lots of money. And since in monopoly capitalism the big corporations are the source of big money, they are also the main sources of political power.'[12] If this were the only evidence for the Marxist contention, it could be replied that there are indeed countervailing sources of money in most of the Western democracies. In particular, organized labour has managed to supply large sums drawn ultimately from the contributions of individual workers. The overwhelming defeat of Senator George McGovern in the US 1972 Presidential campaign could be cited as proof of the dominance of conservative capitalism – since major financial interests were arrayed against him. But his problem was not lack of money. That he managed to collect in large quantities from the contributions of thousands of ordinary people, and without even the normal support typically afforded democratic party candidates by organized labour.

The Marxist claim would have to go deeper into the way in which capitalist power creates vested interests at strategic points in the society – even in organized labour – and that these interests are disproportionately capable of defending themselves against political attack mounted within the democratic system.

There is enough reality in this picture to warrant our including it as a major problem in economic ethics – and we shall have to return to it later. But I do not believe there is enough truth in it to justify the Marxist claims that democratic political institutions are *nothing but* expressions of dominant class interests. It is worth noting that in recent years in every one of the Western democracies significant legislation has been adopted, so to speak, over the dead bodies of major capitalist interests: social welfare legislation, automobile safety laws, labour legislation, anti-pollution legislation, etc. It can be argued that these are 'concessions' designed to keep the masses happy while retaining the basic structure of capitalism intact. Perhaps that is so; but is it not significant that it is felt that such concessions have to be made? Sweezy's comment that moneyed oligarchies, in general, 'prefer democratic to authoritarian government' because 'the stability of the system is enhanced by periodic popular ratifications of oligarchic rule . . . and certain very real dangers to the oligarchy itself of personal or military dictatorship are avoided',[13] probably imputes too much wisdom to the bourgeoisie. But in any event such a statement points beyond itself to political processes and powers which do not derive directly from the moneyed interests themselves.

But even a Marxist like Sweezy does not think it realistic to prepare for revolution in America. ('The answer of traditional Marxian orthodoxy – that the industrial proletariat must eventually rise in revolution against its capitalist oppressors – no longer carries conviction.'[14]) Instead, the real possibilities of revolution are to be found in the Third World. In time this will affect the whole world: 'The drama of our time is the world revolution; it can never come to an end until it has encompassed the whole world.'[15] What should a Christian's attitude be toward the Marxist revolutions in Third World countries? Clearly, many of these countries are not democracies in any credible sense. To criticize the revolutionaries for sponsoring irresponsible grabs for power is beside the point when the existing powers are so irresponsible. And it is well for Western, especially American Christians to remember that their own countries have often supported these oppressive, irresponsible regimes. Marcuse's point seems much more valid in such situations than, say, in Western Europe or America. Nevertheless, a Christian may hold two important criteria before revolutionary movements counted in the name of social justice: First, are they truly a last resort in a situation where non-violent means cannot at all hope to establish social justice? Second, is the revolution truly accepting as one of its dominant goals the establishment and maintenance of a democratic political order? From the Christian stand-point, it is a typical mistake of Marxists to reduce the alternatives to acceptance of an anti-democratic, anti-socialist authoritarianism or forcible establishment of a socialist authoritarianism. This mistake, again, has its origins in the Marxist belief that its own authoritarianism will in time inevitably give way to a non-authoritarian classless society. Has not history already exposed that to be an illusion?

The peculiar case of Czechoslovakia may here be cited, both as a symbol of tyranny and as a sign of hope. The reform movement, which reached its climax in 1968, was of course crushed by Soviet power in August of that year. During the relatively brief period of the 'Prague spring' there was what seemed to be a genuine renaissance of democratic politics, freedom in the arts and literature, and in religion. It was not, in fact, a rejection of socialism either – for the leading slogan of the movement was 'socialism with a human face'. The Soviet invasion was bitterly resented by the majority of the people.[16] Clearly the Soviet Union considered this new freedom a substantial threat, and it was willing to pay the price of crushing it. Christians, who wish to pay respect to the truth, may note that there are two sides to this event, however. One is the Soviet action, illustrating the hard side of Marxism – what Michael Harrington calls 'a utopian terrorism'.[17] But the more hopeful aspect is the fact that the reform movement itself developed in the bosom of the Czech Communist Party, which may illustrate that there are indeed possibilities of uniting socialism with democratic aspirations. We shall want to examine this possibility seriously in the chapter on Democratic Socialism. But in so far as Marxist ideology, as such, provides a justification for censorship, for denial of freedom to organize politically and to propagate deviant political and economic views, and for the grant of monopoly political power to any segment of society, that ideology falls short of the mark.

Marxist Economic Doctrine

When we turn to Marxist economic doctrine we quickly discover some useless baggage. The 'increased misery theory', in accordance with which it was supposed that under capitalism the workers would become more and more impoverished, simply has not worked out. Even the attempt by Karl Kautsky and others to interpret this as increased *relative* deprivation (that is, the workers considered to be worse off relative to the capitalists, though better off relative to their own previous condition) is not persuasive. That really is not what Marx intended; and if it were it would transfer the question out of economics and into the sphere of relative justice – the problem of the social relationship between the workers and the capitalists.

Even the labour theory of value, so long regarded as the keystone of all Marxist economics[18] may not be indispensable to the whole. Generations of non-Marxist economists, who have cheerfully conducted funeral services over Marxists economics using the labour theory of value as the chief text, have been puzzled by the continued liveliness of the corpse. Perhaps Joan Robinson was more correct than they in her judgment that 'no point of substance in Marx's argument depends upon the labour theory of value'.[19] She may also have been correct in her witty interpretation of why Marx and the Marxists have clung so resolutely to the unnecessary theory:

> Voltaire remarked that it is possible to kill a flock of sheep by witchcraft if you give them plenty of arsenic at the same time. The sheep, in this figure, may well stand for the complacent apologists of capitalism; Marx's penetrating insight and bitter hatred of oppression supply the arsenic, while the labour theory of value provides the incantations.[20]

It is, in short, because the labour theory of value is so inextricably entwined with a *moral* theory of value that it cannot be discarded. But Marx's *economic* analysis is based rather upon the contradictions in capitalism. In understanding these, it may be that Marx even did himself a disservice by confusing matters with an inherently ambiguous theory of value.[21]

But what about the rest of economic Marxism?

There are two interrelated aspects of Marxist economic doctrine. There is the analysis of the irrationalities of capitalism and there is the projection of a more rational and humane socialism.

We have already concluded concerning the first that Marxism is not successful as a science of the self-destruction of capitalism. The system may contain serious irrationalities. It may be self-contradictory at any number of points. It may harbour inefficiencies. And it may foster grave injustices. But Marxism has not really made its case that what is alleged to be a basic contradiction between social production and private ownership must inevitably result in revolutionary change and the emergence of a new socialist, classless society. Nevertheless, the problems in capitalism which have been exposed by Marxism cannot be overlooked. What are we to say about the periodic economic crises in the trade cycle, when vast numbers of perfectly willing workers are thrown out of work and factories with great productive capacity are idle? Is there not more than just a little plausibility in the Marxist assertion that the workers are not employed and the plants cannot operate because management cannot anticipate making a profit? And is this not because of the form of ownership? And how are we to evaluate the apparent need of a capitalist society to stimulate, through advertising, the desire to purchase unnecessary, trivial, and even harmful products? And how are we to justify the vast expenditures of wealth upon perfectly unnecessary (from the viewpoint of social benefit) functions in the community: the advertising hucksters, unnecessary middle-men, insurance programmes, and so on? What are we to say for a system that provides a serious economic reason for manufacturers to build obsolescence into their products – either in terms of style changes or through unnecessary wearing out of essential parts? What, finally, are we to say about the building of society that institutionalizes and fosters greed?

Such questions as these are, of course, highly provocative. One can imagine an intelligent defender of capitalism fairly leaping to his feet to challenge the assumptions which lie behind these questions. Which means that we cannot finally dispose of the Marxist indictment of capitalism, one way or the other, until we have had a look at capitalism's own ideological claims. So this must be postponed to the next chapter.

Meanwhile, however, a few provisional things can be said concerning the Marxists's own economic vision of the classless society based upon socialism. For the strictly moral standpoint, that vision has much to commend it. It certainly takes the central Christian values outlined in Chapter 3 quite seriously. It is based upon equality. It seeks an economic undergirding of real human unity – an economic basis for the realization of human family as a family. It is concerned, both morally and economically, with the creative possibilities of every human member of the community and, in this sense, respects the value of each person. It takes production seriously and desires the material progress of economic life – not for materialistic reasons *per se* but because of the benefits this progress will mean in the further liberation of the human spirit. It even provides a basis for dealing rationally with the environmental problems occasioned by too rapid economic growth and the selfish plundering of the resources of earth for private gain.

This is the vision, and it is not a bad one. We are immediately reminded that socialist practice has not worked out exactly in this fashion. There remain vast inequalities in all socialist countries (the 'new class'). Private consumption, which might provide more of the economic liberation of individuals through labour-saving appliances, culturally enriching facilities, and automobiles, has been permitted to lag. Vast sums are put into defence. And even the rivers and air are polluted, just like the capitalist countries. These realities are not irrelevant. But over the long run, we have to ask every ideology where its dominant interests and motives lie. Are they in the direction of a broader vision of human fulfilment or are they in the direction of forces that the ultimately wasteful and divisive? Moreover, there is the terribly important question of the extent to which it is necessary to tolerate some evils in the form of economic organization in order to achieve what is in the long run likely to be the greater good.

These questions, too, cannot really be faced until we turn to the counter-claims of laissez faire capitalism.

In sum, then, we can regard the Marxist conception of alienation as offering us great insight into what is ultimately at stake in economic life. At the same time, this enduring contribution of Marxist ideology is accompanied by serious flaws in its appraisal of the sources of human evil and its consequent blind spot toward evils in the revolutionary and post-revolutionary situation. Economic questions remain which can only be addressed as we take up laissez faire capitalism.

5

The Case for Laissez Faire Capitalism

> Few trends would so thoroughly undermine the very foundations of our free society as the acceptance by corporate officials of a social responsibility other than to make as much money for their stockholders as they possibly can.
>
> Milton Friedman (1962)

We have already had a preliminary look at the intellectual scheme that underlies this kind of remark. The idea that this scheme is above ideology has already been rejected. It may have some basis in economic science, but as a whole it is a mixture of value judgments with a certain model of how economic life really functions. We must here examine both. Strictly speaking, laissez faire capitalism is the doctrine that the self-regulating market economy should be left almost entirely alone. This is 'pure' capitalism, with only that minimum of governmental interference required to protect the economy from interferences. Such an extreme capitalist position is widely regarded today as obsolete, and some may wonder why it is necessary to devote an entire chapter to it. The reason is that laissez faire, no matter how much it may seem discredited in some quarters, is still a very live force in Western economic thinking. Those who believe in it most strongly may, if they are in authority make compromises for practical reasons. But their governing presumption is still for a 'hands-off' attitude towards free market capitalism. Any governmental regulations or governmental spending and taxation must bear the burden of proof. Moreover, even if laissez faire did not have a following, the case for that ideology raises many important value questions which we can scarcely by-pass.

The Miracle of the Self-Regulating Market

The central claim of laissez faire capitalism is that the free enterprise market does a better job of regulating itself than any authority could possibly do. It can do a better job from a practical standpoint, and the most important human values will best be safeguarded through this mechanism. The self-regulating market can be described as a 'miracle' because it co-ordinates the activities and decisions of vast numbers of individuals and enterprises efficiently even though no individual or co-ordinating authority could possibly have direct knowledge of all the complex details.

Expressed very simply, the theory is that each person (or enterprise) is free either to buy or to sell on the open market. Each buyer will buy at the lowest possible price, each seller will sell at the highest possible price. (This is true of human labour, just as it is of tangible commodities.) It will always pay to make and sell the things that people are most interested in buying. If there is not very much demand for a particular product, producers will have to stop making it and turn instead to making things that people want to buy. Thus, the market will 'signal' producers that it doesn't want this to be produced, but it does want that. If an enterprise cannot adjust to such changes in the market it will go out of business, and the workers and productive resources it has been using will be available to be used by enterprises that are more responsive to consumer demand. Prices will tend to fall under competitive conditions, for each enterprise – in order to sell its products and make a profit – will try to produce its goods more cheaply in order to underbid the competition. Thus, also, there is the most intense kind of pressure to cut costs – that is to say, to produce more and more efficiently. The 'discipline of the market' thus helps to assure the responsiveness of the whole economy to the people who count, the consumers, and at the same time to enforce the most efficient possible kinds of production.

The free market has also encouraged people to save, to defer their own consumption and pool their resources in order to invest in more and more productive machinery and factories. By permitting people to accumulate private wealth, the system motivates them to keep enlarging the productive capacity of the whole society. The 'profit motive', while it may appear selfish, leads ultimately to greater productivity and wealth for all. Those who are most thrifty and most productive receive their due reward for their services to all.

Everybody agrees that capitalism, whatever its problems, has been tremendously productive. Von Mises, who rarely understates this achievement, has this to say:

> Although continually sabotaged by the folly and the malice of the masses and the ideological remnants of the precapitalistic methods of thinking and acting, free enterprise has radically changed the fate of man. It has reduced mortality rates and prolonged the average length of life, thus multiplying population figures. It has, in an unprecedented way, raised the standard of living of the average man in those nations that did not too severely impede the acquisitive spirit of enterprising individuals. All people, however fanatical they may be in their zeal to disparage and to fight capitalism, implicitly pay homage to it by passionately clamoring for the products it turns out.
>
> The wealth capitalism has brought to mankind is not an achievement of a mythical force called progress. . . . What transformed the stagnant conditions of the good old days into the activism of capitalism was not changes in the natural sciences and in technology, but the adoption of the free enterprise principle.[1]

One does not have to take von Mises' word for it when Marx and Engels say the same thing, and with scarcely less enthusiasm. The bourgeoisie, they write in the *Communist Manifesto*,

> Has been the first to show what man's activity can bring about. It has accomplished wonders far surpassing Egyptian pyramids, Roman aqueducts, and Gothic cathedrals; it has conducted expeditions that put in the shade all former exoduses of nations and crusades.[2]

Even the obvious point that capitalism has done all this at the cost of periodic crises, recessions, and depressions may not carry as much weight as the critics of capitalism suppose. Joseph A. Schumpeter, who was not a laissez faire ideologue, pointed out that the productive accomplishments of capitalism need to be seen over the long run of several decades in order to be fully appreciated. Despite all the fluctuations of the business cycle (including the serious depression of 1873–1877), Schumpeter was able to show that total output of the American economy available for consumption increased by 2% compounded annually for each year from 1870 to 1930.[3] This was during the period of most unrestrained free enterprise in American history. Total available output from 1930–1976, computed on the same basis, has been 3% per year. Governmental assistance or interference, depending on one's point of view, has been much greater in these years, of course. Laissez faire advocates like von Mises would say that continuing productive progress has been in spite of this governmental involvement, not because of it. That judgment, as we have already suggested in Chapter 2, could not be supported. But the dynamics of the free market could still be credited with much of this continuing productive growth. John C. Bennett, who is by no means an advocate of laissez faire, has for this kind of reason cited the 'creative dynamism' of capitalism as one of its ethically positive features: 'The energies that capitalism has stimulated because of its use of the profit incentive have led to the great benefits as well as to the many ills of modern society. On balance this process has surely been constructive.'[4]

Freedom and Distributive Justice in Capitalism

In so far as productive efficiency can be related to positive ethical values, then, laissez faire capitalism can make important claims: it increases the sum total of products for consumption, and it apparently does so faster than alternative economic systems. More will be said later concerning social costs and social consumption. But it should be remarked here that rapid expansion of personal consumption is potentially of great value to humanity. Many, but not all, of the products which have become available in the past century or two of capitalism are of inestimable value in liberating the human spirit from undesirable constraints of the natural world. Think of the revolutions in agricultural productivity, in medical technology, in communication, transportation, and housing. These advances should not be treated as gods, but they surely serve to better the human condition.

Apart from this, the ideology of laissez faire has tended to emphasize two main values: freedom and distributive justice, both of which are given a characteristic interpretation.

The Chicago economist, Milton Friedman, has dealt with the first of these most persuasively. 'As liberals', he writes, 'we take freedom of the individual, or perhaps the family, as our ultimate goal in judging social arrangements.'[5] This is not simply a matter of economics. In his opinion this is the crucial value on the basis of which economic systems have to be judged. Indeed, Friedman argues in effect that there can be no such thing as ethics apart from the elbow room an individual is given by his society to follow the dictates of his conscience. Society should not try to take the key ethical decisions out of the individual's hands: '... a major aim of the liberal is to leave the ethical problem for the individual to wrestle with. The 'really' important ethical problems are those that face an individual in a free society – what he should do with his freedom.'[6]

Thus, Friedman is not at all opposed to altruism. But it should be the altruism of free individuals, not that of the state acting in their behalf. Nor, as the quotation at the beginning of this chapter suggests, should responsible corporate leaders abuse their powers by treating their enterprises as social welfare institutions.

This conception of freedom is closely associated in Friedman's thinking with a particular approach to distributive justice. People should be required to pay for the things they consume. Otherwise, they will, in effect, be taking things from others. The point is both moral and economic in its significance. From the moral standpoint, it is simply unfair that people be deprived of their goods against their will. From an economic standpoint, it is only possible to maintain the system of market pricing if people are required to buy the things they want to have and to use. Friedman goes to great lengths to observe this doctrine: benefits such as schools, parks, highways should be paid for directly by the users. Only in the case of benefits having a 'neighbourhood effect' – that is, when it is impossible to determine the extent to which any particular person benefits directly – can we legitimately charge the service to the whole community. He includes some urban parks in this category, although national parks could be handled as a personal benefit that people pay for directly.

Both conceptions – of freedom and of distributive justice – are united in the contractual theory of society which is generally accepted by Friedman, von Mises, and other supporters of laissez faire. The central notion is that people find their social fulfilment through free exchange. Voluntary co-operation is the ethical model of community. Friedman will go so far as to say that everybody benefits from all voluntary exchanges: 'both parties to an economic transaction benefit from it, *provided the transaction is bilaterally voluntary and informed*.'[7] Von Mises says it even more strongly:

> . . . the fundamental principle of collective action is the mutual exchanges of services, the *do ut des*. The individual gives and serves in order to be rewarded by his fellow men's gifts and services. He gives away what he values less in order to receive something that at the moment of the transaction he considers as more desirable. He exchanges– buys or sells – because he thinks that this is the most advantageous thing he can do at the time.[8]

Of course, it may occur to the reader that in *this* sense the payment of blackmail or ransom money is a beneficial exchange of services – so Friedman's way of putting it may do the laissez faire cause more good.

It should finally be noted here that, while laissez faire has generally been opposed to all social welfare legislation, Milton Friedman and a few others have attempted to provide for the necessary minimum of governmental welfare programmes with least disruption of the mechanisms of the market place. Recognizing that many people are the helpless victims of circumstance, Friedman was one of the first to suggest a comprehensive national negative income tax programme – a variation of the guaranteed annual income idea. While the programme would include work incentives by permitting recipients to retain some portion of their earned income, it would guarantee a basic minimum income for all persons in society. Thus, everybody would have access to the market, even if unable to provide a socially saleable product or service. This basic income grant would replace all existing welfare programmes, including social casework and provision of housing or food in kind.

The 'Protestant Ethic'

Many readers will recognize the connection between these ideas and the so-called 'Protestant ethic'. That term, taken from Max Weber's classical study of the relationship between Calvinism and the emergence of Western capitalism,[9] refers to the strong Protestant emphasis upon the value of work and the notion that people should receive what they deserve. Undoubtedly, the Calvinist strain in the cultural development of Switzerland and the Anglo-Saxon countries has had some effect in supporting the ethical claims of the laissez faire ideology, although it should immediately be noted that that ideology falls short of the real Protestant ethic at two decisive points. In the first place, the genuine emphasis of Calvinism always had a much deeper commitment to the life of the community. Calvin and the greatest of his followers would have been appalled by the extremes to which laissez faire capitalism carried individualism. In the second place, the early Protestants would have objected strongly to the implied self-righteousness of the laissez faire idea of deserving. Ultimately, the Protestant reformers would have said, what we *deserve* is damnation! It is only by the grace of God that we have the possibility of real fulfilment as human beings; to speak of 'deserving' so casually implies that we are capable of saving ourselves.

These points have great importance in our overall evaluation of laissez faire capitalism, and we shall return to them later.

The Problem of the 'Profit Motive'

It is obvious that laissez faire ideology has not the slightest hesitation in appealing directly and frankly to what has loosely been called the 'profit motive'.[10] Most writers consider this an asset, not a liability. Some, such as Ayn Rand, go to considerable extremes in glorifying the 'virtue of selfishness'[11] contrasting this with a lifeless, self-contradictory altruism. Others, taking note of the near-universality of selfish drives, argue that it is better to put such drives to work for the betterment of society than it is to allow self-centred people to enslave others or tear the community apart with conflict.

This is an interesting point which has not usually been understood fully by the critics of laissez faire. Von Mises, the real philosopher of laissez faire, makes it best. Noting that some people have a good deal more ability and drive than others, von Mises argues that the best system will be the one that literally requires even the most selfish of such people to serve their brethren if they expect to get ahead. Thus,

> by the instrumentality of the profit-and-loss system, the most eminent members of society are prompted to serve to the best of their abilities the well-being of the masses of less gifted people. What pays under capitalism is satisfying the common man, the customer. The more people you satisfy, the better for you.[12]

'This system', he continues, 'is certainly not ideal. . . . But the only alternative to it is the totalitarian system, in which in the name of a fictitious entity, "society", a group of directors determines the fate of all the people.'

Von Mises also remarks that the free market does not necessarily presuppose selfishness. In the determination of market prices, it does not matter 'whether an "egotistic" buyer buys because he wants himself to enjoy what he bought or whether an "altruistic" buyer buys for some other reasons, for instance in order to make a gift to a charitable institution.'[13] The point is that the buyer is seeking satisfaction, and the actual motive guiding him to satisfaction may be quite unselfish. But, whether or not people are unselfish, the system has made provision for the 'worst case' – that is, even if the worst things about human nature gain ascendancy, *this* system translates that selfishness into the greater good.

This way of *stating* it is, I submit, a good deal more refined than Adam Smith. And it certainly goes beyond the typical stereotype of laissez faire capitalism and its 'profit motive'. The problem is whether that is really how things work. Two dissenting voices are worth hearing while we are on the subject.

The first, Joan Robinson, observes quite sagely that 'if the pursuit of profit is the criterion of proper behaviour there is no way of distinguishing between productive activity and robbery'.[14] She quotes from an interview with Al Capone in which the gangster shouted 'This American system of ours, call it Americanism, call it Capitalism, call it what you like, gives to each and every one of us a great opportunity if we only seize it with both hands and make the most of it.' Professor Robinson's point is that if we dignify selfish motives too much they can easily explode beyond the bounds of any system.

The other critic, John Bennett, states the problem as a moral dilemma.

> The profit motive as a subjective phenomenon, unless it is very much limited and tamed, is morally objectionable. It tends to corrupt the individual and it becomes the source of temptation, even in far-reaching decisions, to put a very limited interest before the common good. The profit system, in so far as it is a stimulus to initiative and in so far as it provides moments of truth with the prospect of profit or loss by which institutions are shaken out of ruts, is on balance a constructive force. Yet the profit system can easily over-stimulate the profit motive as personal acquisitiveness and thus it becomes morally problematic. This is a moral dilemma that is built into capitalism; it requires both internal disciplines within the system and external checks.[15]

There is one further problem with the 'profit motive' which may present us with the supreme irony of economic ethics. In so far as this 'motive' is basically competitive, it may also be dehumanizing. That is to say, if one's economic drive represents the desire for a higher status than one's fellows, it is a drive toward isolation. In a Christian perspective, the paradoxical effect of our quest for human fulfilment through higher status may well be loss of human fulfilment through spiritual separation. Putting this more bluntly, we had better not dignify ordinary selfishness too much lest we have to learn again the hard way that selfishness disintegrates both individual and corporate life.

Poverty and Inequality in Capitalism

From the very beginning of capitalism there has been an intense debate over whether the system of laissez faire creates more poverty or whether it alleviates it. Baron and Sweezy speak for the critics: 'as Marx pointed out in *Capital* and as the experience of the subsequent century of capitalist development has confirmed again and again, capitalism everywhere generates wealth at one pole and poverty at the other.'[16] This 'law of capitalist development' means that large numbers of people live below the subsistence minimum, while others continue to grow wealthier and wealthier. Even today, according to these authors, almost half the people in the United States live below this subsistence minimum. To arrive at this estimate, Baron and Sweezy have used the US Government's own definition of a minimum subsistence income – subsistence being understood as the level below which one cannot function normally in modern society.

Against this, capitalist writers have always emphasized the cornucopia of benefits that capitalist production has poured out upon all. Even 'poor' people in America are incredibly rich by world standards. US Steel Chairman Roger Blough, no enemy of capitalism, writes to 'deplore . . . the fact that several million American families have incomes of less than three thousand dollars a year'. But he goes on to note that 'to more than half the families on earth today an income equivalent to three thousand dollars a year would represent undreamed of affluence. So although they are classified as 'poor' by government definition, it does not mean that these American families are hungry, homeless or unclothed.' He continues,

> In fact, census data show that three out of four of the so-called poor own a washing machine; while more than half have both a television and a telephone, 20 per cent own a home freezer and one out of seven bought an automobile last year.[17]

These points can be conceded. In fact, since Blough wrote these words the percentages of poor people owning washing machines, television sets and automobiles have risen. So why the debate?

It is not that one side or the other in this dispute is wrong or stupid. It is largely a question of definition. Granted that some people even in America, the richest country on earth, actually do suffer serious deprivation and do not have adequate food, clothing or shelter, the real issue isn't this. The real issue is what is happening to people in *relative* terms. Both the critics and friends of capitalism could readily agree that *relatively* there are vast discrepancies between the poor and the rich in this system. The question is whether this matters. The laissez faire capitalist is likely to say that the important thing is not to divide the pie more equally. If we do this, we will not make the pie grow, and we may even make it get smaller and smaller through our neglect of the only system that increases productivity. Many laissez faire advocates consider equality to be both undesirable and impossible as a social ideal. In one book, von Mises insists that 'men are unequal; individuals differ from one another. They differ because their prenatal as well as their postnatal history is never identical.'[18] In another he writes that,

> Nothing . . . is ill-founded as the assertion of the alleged equality of all members of the human race. Men are altogether unequal. Even between brothers there exist the most marked differences in physical and mental attributes. Nature never repeats itself in its creations; it produces nothing by the dozen, nor are its products standardized. Each man who leaves her workshop bears the imprint of the individual, the unique, the never-to-recur. Men are not equal, and the demand for equality under the law can by no means be grounded in the contention that equal treatment is due to equals.[19]

He goes on to support equality under law for prudential reasons, but this is not to be confused with any form of economic equality.

What has happened in this debate, of course, is that the supporters of laissez faire have insisted that only *absolute* poverty constitutes a moral problem. Here, we must side with the critics who argue that *relative* poverty is also important morally. A case can possibly be made for inequality as a 'lesser evil' required by incentives for production. But this is still a lesser *evil*. Inequality is an evil because it divides the community and has a serious tendency to create distinctions between 'superior' and 'inferior' people. Such distinctions might not concern von Mises in the slightest, but they run contrary to the basic Christian values we have already considered.

Still, this may not leave us with an open-and-shut case against the free enterprise system. It will come as a surprise to some readers to discover that some serious economists have concluded that, in the long run, capitalism has been and will be an *equalizer*. Friedman make this claim: 'capitalism leads to less inequality than alternative systems of organization and . . . the development of capitalism has greatly lessened the extent of inequality.' Since

Friedman is known to be to the right of Adam Smith anyway, we should recall that the more circumspect economist Joseph Schumpeter arrived at essentially the same conclusion – but for different reasons. Schumpeter noted that relative shares of national income had, at his time of writing in 1950, remained fairly constant for the previous one hundred years. (In purely statistical terms, the past quarter of a century from 1950 to 1975 has not changed this picture much.) But this is income measured in money terms. If we are thinking of actual consumption, 'relative shares have substantially changed in favour of the lower income groups'. How could Schumpeter have arrived at this curious judgment? His argument is worth repeating in his own words:

> This follows from the fact that the capitalist engine is first and last an engine of mass production which unavoidably means also production for the masses, whereas, climbing upward in the scale of individual incomes, we find that an increasing proportion is being spent on personal services and on handmade commodities, the prices of which are largely a function of wages rates.[20]

This is the economic principle. He goes on to illustrate what this actually means.

> There are no doubt some things available to the modern workman that Louis XIV himself would have been delighted to have yet was unable to have – modern dentistry for instance. On the whole, however, a budget on that level had little that really mattered to gain from capitalist achievement. Even speed of travelling may be assumed to have been a minor consideration for so very dignified a gentleman. Electric lighting is no great boon to anyone who has money enough to buy a sufficient number of candles and to pay servants to attend to them. It is the cheap cloth, the cheap cotton and rayon fabric, boots, motorcars and so on that are the typical achievements of capitalist production, and not as a rule improvements that would mean much to the rich man. Queen Elizabeth owned silk stockings. The capitalist achievement does not typically consist in providing more silk stockings for queens but in bringing them within the reach of factory girls in return for steadily decreasing amounts of effort. . . the capitalist process, not by coincidence but by virtue of its mechanism, progressively raises the standard of life of the masses.

This is quite an impressive argument, and every critic of capitalism ought to reflect upon it seriously. This is not just the 'enlarge the pie' argument typically used. Schumpeter is really saying that the inescapable tendency of this kind of production is to overcome not only 'absolute' poverty but 'relative' poverty as well. Not in money terms, to be sure; but in terms of those aspects of material life which count in social relationships as well. Fewer and fewer material things can function unambiguously as real status symbols. There may be considerable differences in the quality of material and craftsmanship in a fine hand-tailored suit and something off the rack at J. C. Penney's or Burton's. But one can get by socially quite well with the latter as well as the former. The same thing can be said about automobiles, furniture, books, food. Indeed, there is a kind of reverse status symbol in demonstrating one's psychological independence by deliberately using cheaper mass-produced items that are functionally quite adequate. In some circles one must, above all else, avoid ostentation.[21]

Before we let our enthusiasm for egalitarian capitalism get out of hand, we need to remember that without a good deal of governmental interference even this mass-produced paradise would not be possible. For production under laissez faire conditions cannot occur without a market, and it has been shown to the satisfaction of most economists that a substantial involvement by government is necessary to sustain market demand. In particular, we should now make note of the fact that a purely laissez faire economy would leave some people out altogether. If our purchasing power derives finally only from income we have gained through selling something (products or labour), then the market is a pretty grim place for people who need to buy but have nothing to sell. In America, despite the existence of social welfare programmes that go far beyond the limits of laissez faire, there are still 24 million people with family incomes below $5,100 per year (the 1976 poverty line for a family of four). Mass production may indeed have real egalitarian effects. But it is no help at all to people who haven't the cash to buy the products.

The point was brought home to me by examining the poverty statistics for the decade 1960–1969. This period is a useful one to study because of the number and variety of anti-poverty programmes. At the beginning of the decade there were, according to governmental definition, about 33 million poor people in America. By the end, the number had been reduced to 24 million.

Since most of the anti-poverty programmes emphasized work-training schemes of one kind or another and since the decade also witnessed a developing economic boom, the figures provide some measure of what can be done if we maximize the number of people who can earn an income. The results are not unimpressive. But upon closer examination we notice certain categories of people who were not helped at all. We see in particular that families headed by single women (usually widowed, divorced, or separated) have scarcely been affected at all (10.4 million in 1959, 10.5 million in 1969). Of course there are also the aged, the disabled, the mentally incompetent, etc. who cannot benefit much from capitalistic production unless they are *given* a passport (money) to the marketplace.

Most people recognize this, which is why most of the capitalistic countries have social welfare programmes and income support. But the laissez faire purists haven't even yet taken the point. (In so far as Milton Friedman, through his proposal of a minimum negative income tax, is an exception to this charge he is also a deviant from the pure laissez faire ideology. And even Friedman doesn't want to give the poor very much!) In the 'democracy of the marketplace' where the consumer reigns supreme, some people have vastly more votes than others.

So, while not overlooking the truth of the claims made by Schumpeter and others, we must conclude that a purely laissez faire economy would not be very egalitarian.

Laissez Faire and Democracy

One of the main problems we noted with Marxism is its effect in undermining support for democratic political institutions. What about laissez faire?

From the beginning of capitalism, the ideology of laissez faire has tended to coincide with that of political democracy. With both the byword is freedom. Contemporary supporters of laissez faire continue to emphasize the connection. Sometimes the claims seem exaggerated. Thus Friedman:

> Historical evidence speaks with a single voice on the relation between freedom and a free market. I know of no example in time or place of a society that has been marked by a large measure of

political freedom, and that has not also used something comparable to a free market to organize the bulk of economic activity. .... History suggests ... that capitalism is a necessary condition for political freedom.[22]

Thus also von Mises:

> The foundation of Western bourgeois civilization is the economic system of capitalism, the political corollary of which is representative government and freedom of thought and interpersonal communication.... It was in the climate created by this capitalistic system of individualism that all the modern intellectual achievements thrived. Never before had mankind lived under conditions like those of the second part of the nineteenth century, when, in the civilized countries, the most momentous problems of philosophy, religion, and science could be freely discussed without any fear of reprisals on the part of the powers that be.[23]

Marxists, as we have seen, consider this to be quite absurd. The 'freedom' is the freedom to live by the capitalistic rules; and as for representative democracy, it mainly represents moneyed interests. But that, too, is not necessarily the case.

Perhaps we can simply say that democracy is *possible* under a laissez faire system. So long as the whole system's commitment to freedom is genuine, it may even be a supportive factor. On the other hand, it should be fairly obvious that great concentrations of wealth have always influenced democratic process disproportionately. Even von Mises indulges a bit of elitism in his attitude toward the masses which betrays something less than a full commitment to democracy: 'The inferiority of the multitude manifests itself most convincingly in the fact that they loathe the capitalistic system and stigmatize the profits that their own behaviour creates as unfair.'[24] The 'democracy of the market', which von Mises clearly considers more important than the political one, 'brings about ... a state of affairs in which production activities are operated by those of whose conduct of affairs the masses approve by buying their products'. Those who rise to the top in economic matters are perhaps more suited to govern than their inferior brethren, and if so, the disproportionate political power of wealth would be no offence to von Mises' viewpoint. It is all reminiscent of Andrew Carnegie and others of the American robber baron era who sincerely believed that the best men of the age were those who controlled the wealth and that such people ought to be permitted to run things.

It is striking that people like Friedman and von Hayek and von Mises – for all their strong affirmations of freedom, democracy, etc. – insist upon the 'market ballot's' priority to the political ballot. The free market is the fundamental institution. Political democracy, happily, is a corollary. But these thinkers are not, we recall, concerned in the slightest about the inequalities of marketplace balloting. Their marketplace democracy is accordingly still a weighted, aristocratic one – although they would claim that the aristocracy is one of merit and not one of birth. (On this point Carnegie was more consistent since he recognized the effects of inheritance and urged that it should not be allowed.) To this extent, then, their vision of political democracy is unfortunately clouded.

Moreover, the seemingly absolute commitment to consumer decision-making inevitably stacks the cards against collective market activity: that is, buying and selling conducted by society *as a whole*. Only the political ballot ultimately can control collective expenditure democratically. The difficulty in doing this is no problem to believers in laissez faire because they wish to keep public taxing and spending to an absolute minimum. But those who feel more strongly about the importance of governmental economic activity may believe that laissez faire's democratic government is impotent to translate the will of the people into meaningful action on the issues that matter.

Laissez faire cannot protest against this that the market is a better indication of that will of the people. Because of the way the market is organized its 'message' is by definition restricted to information about what individuals and voluntary associations want to buy. Its bias is heavily in favour of private consumer goods. How, indeed, could the private enterprise market tell us a thing about what the majority of the community would like to have by way of schools, highways, airports, parks? Perhaps this is why Friedman is so insistent that as many of these things as possible should be handled only through the market. Remembering, as we must, that that market is not an equal market, we are bound to conclude that this is a strange kind of democracy indeed. In the deeper ethical perspective, it is clear that this ideology is terribly confused about how the whole community must take counsel together concerning the basic conditions of its historical existence. The market is not a broad enough institution to encompass all of the decisions that have to be made affecting human welfare.

The Problem of Social Costs

This point is dramatically clear in relation to the undistributed social costs of private enterprise. Who pays for the polluted lakes and rivers, the befouled air and resultant medical treatment for emphysema, the disruption of peace and quiet resulting from jet aircraft, etc.? If the advocates of laissez faire were fully logical they would be the first to insist that every productive enterprise must be restrained from fouling the air and water and sound waves of others or that they should bear the full cost of public abatement of these problems. This is not only a question of democratic control and fairness, it is also a question of accuracy in cost accounting. When an enterprise dumps its refuse into the atmosphere and rivers which are the common property of the entire community, it is asking the entire community to assume some of its costs.[25] Yet we all know that the ecology movement has had to struggle upstream against the determined resistance of many capitalists.

From the cost accounting standpoint, the same principle could be made to apply in reverse in the case of educational benefits, public health, highways, harbours, etc. which benefit corporate enterprises. These things are social benefits which are enjoyed by particular industrial enterprises at public expense. My point is not to condemn public expense in these matters, but only to suggest that all of this should be open to public legislation and administration. The ideological implications of this problem will be dealt with more fully in a subsequent chapter.

The Accumulation of Wealth

Much of the chapter thus far may have seemed to have skirted around one of the most fundamental issues posed by laissez faire capitalism: the immense and growing inequality of wealth. We have already seen that inequalities of income under capitalism are mitigated by the equalizing tendencies of mass production itself. But what about the masses of wealth that are meanwhile accumulating disproportionately in the hands of the few? To illustrate the problem, a *Fortune* magazine study in 1968 reported that some 153 individuals each had total wealth greater than $100 million (the list was headed by billionaires J. P. Getty and Howard Hughes and included several with assets above half a billion).[26] Other studies have shown that 1.6% of the adult population in America holds at least 30% of the wealth.[27] The basic distribution of wealth at the top has remained essentially the same for the past quarter of a century. Clearly there is little ground to expect wealth to become more evenly distributed, and under a laissez faire economy there would be no ground to expect this at all.

That is of course exactly the problem that Marxism has pointed to with its concept of surplus value. Wealth created by workers is skimmed off by the capitalist in the form of private wealth.

To be sure, not all this wealth is such that it *could* be consumed privately. Most of it consists of factories and transportation facilities and the like. A capitalist can always sell his shares and use the money for luxury goods. But, if every capitalist tried to do this at once there would be no buyers and the vast accumulation of productive wealth would not be usable privately. John Maynard Keynes, with humorous insight spoke of the basic fiction involved in this situation. The workers, according to Keynes, were willing to accept only a small part of the cake they have produced and the capitalists 'were allowed to call the best part of the cake theirs and were theoretically free to consume it, on the tacit underlying condition that they consumed very little of it in practice. The duty of 'saving' became nine-tenths of virtue and the growth of the cake the object of true religion.' The virtue of the cake, he continued, was 'that it was never to be consumed, neither by you or your children after you'.[28] To put the matter more strongly, as the laissez faire capitalist would undoubtedly want to do, the wealth of the capitalist is held *in trust*. It is, in fact, an immense service to the workers that there are capitalists who are willing to accumulate and manage productive wealth in this way – for otherwise where would all the jobs be, and how could the workers themselves benefit from the tremendous increases in economic productivity which have come with capitalism?

Now that we have had a look at both the Marxist and laissez faire interpretations of capitalistic wealth, we can imagine a conversation between representatives of these ideologies on the question of capital accumulation. It might run something like this:

Marxist: Capitalism exploits the workers. Profits are surplus value produced by workers but stolen from them by capitalists.

Capitalist: The term 'surplus value' begs the question, but never mind that. What is taken by the capitalist as profit is mainly for *investment*. It is private property, but it is for the sake of production. It would be the same thing objectively speaking even if it were owned by the public. After all, don't the socialist countries have to keep back some of the wealth for further expansion of production? Why don't you call that 'surplus value' and 'exploitation'?

Marxist: You forget that those top wealth holders live like kings! They certainly *can* consume wealth – at least a lot more of it than the workers. But even if we assume (for the sake of argument) that wealthy capitalists live at the same level as the workers you overlook the crucial problem: private owners have all the economic *power*. They alone are in a position to decide what is to be produced and when and where, and they alone decide who is to be employed.

Capitalist: I will concede your first point, that successful capitalists enjoy a higher standard of living. This is a necessary incentive for the capitalist to put his abilities to work for society. Your second point just isn't accurate. It isn't the owner of capital who has the power, it is the consumer. The capitalist supplies the productive power and the business sense that responds to market demand. The owner, for the sake of his incentive-reward, serves as an efficient middle-man. He is the servant of the consumer. If he does this poorly he will be punished by losing some or all of his capital.

Marxist: This may be *somewhat* true – if we could ignore monopoly price-fixing, manipulation by advertising, planned obsolescence, collusion among manufacturers to limit production, and other devices of consumer manipulation. But even if it were entirely true that the capitalist is the 'servant' of the consumer, this only begs the question of power. For consumer power only represents a partial interest of society, not the whole interest. The whole interest includes what can be called public goods. Private capital, under pure capitalism, retains the right to determine *that* as well. The market is not a very good mechanism for determining social consumption because it is private and individualistic.

Capitalist: Of course it is private and individualistic. If decision making is to be democratic, it must be based on private, individual power. What could be more democratic? The market is a democratic institution.

Marxist: You forget that the private, individual power is very unevenly developed. Some have vastly more dollar-or-pound-votes than do others. Even if that were not so, you miss my point. The individualism of the market, whether or not it is 'democratic', is appropriate to private consumption – not to public expenditures for needed public goods and services.

We can safely abandon our imaginary conversation at this point, assured that the last word has not been spoken by either party. If we were to spin out such a conversation to encompass all of the points at issue between Marxism and laissez faire capitalism, it might become clear that both have enduring contributions to make but at the same time that neither is able to satisfy us.

We may summarize the enduring contributions of laissez faire as including (1) awareness of the importance of economic freedom and creativity, allowing for the maximum feasible initiative by individuals and groups, (2) the market mechanism which, with all regard for its imperfections, provides useful economic stimulus and effective structures for cost accounting and allocation of resources, and (3) concern for the benefits of private consumption.

All three of these are positive benefits. But taken as a whole and incorporated into an absolute system of laissez faire, they create a terrible blindness to the effects of greed and the anarchy of unco-ordinated economic activity. They also erode the foundations of political democracy by depriving political institutions of the power to act on behalf of the whole community on the economic problems which may affect the community most – despite the strong affirmations of the importance of freedom and representative government. Finally, they may be blind to the importance of conservation for future generations and to the intangible beauties of life which are not reducible to the cash nexus of the marketplace.

In sum, the miraculous market mechanism may be a good servant, but it is almost certainly a bad master.

Speaking to the debate between laissez faire capitalism and Marxian Communism, the first Assembly of the World Council of Churches called upon the churches to reject both these ideologies and to look beyond them toward more promising alternatives:

> Each has made promises which it could not redeem. Communist ideology puts the emphasis upon economic justice, and promises that freedom will come automatically after the completion of the revolution. Capitalism puts the emphasis upon freedom, and promises that justice will follow as a byproduct of free enterprise; that, too, is an ideology which has been proved false. It is the responsibility of Christians to seek new, creative solutions which never allow either justice or freedom to destroy the other.

From the Christian moral standpoint, the real options are more likely to be found in the emerging debate over democratic socialism and what can be called social market capitalism. We shall examine the possibilities of these ideological approaches in the following two chapters.

6

The Case for Social Market Capitalism

> There is simply no other choice than this: either to abstain from interference in the free play of the market, or to delegate the entire management of production and distribution to the government. Either capitalism or socialism: there exists no middle way.
>
> Ludwig von Mises

As we have seen, von Mises believes there *really* is only the one choice of capitalism. But apart from this, any good Marxist might well accept the above way of formulating the alternatives. Perhaps we have already delved sufficiently into the extremes of Marxism and laissez faire to see that, whatever their undoubted merits, neither ideology is a suitable vehicle, taken by itself, for Christian economic thinking. In comparison, the 'mixed economy' option is undoubtedly formidable. What could von Mises (or a Marxist) say in response to Paul Samuelson's simple claim: 'The fruits of post-Keynesian economics have been the better working of the mixed economy. The era since World War II has witnessed a world growth in output and living standards unmatched in recorded history.'[1]? Of course, much can be said, pro and con, about the actual effects of the mixed economy during the post-World War II era of its flowering. But first, we must have a look at the ideology underlying this remarkable development.

The Theory of Social Market

In the last chapter I remarked that the free market is potentially a useful servant although it is almost certainly a bad master. Social market capitalism is, in effect, based upon this principle. Those who support this 'mixed economy' conception do so out of conviction that the capitalistic market apparatus is an immensely productive tool. But they are also convinced that this tool needs to be harnessed to social objectives determined outside the marketplace itself. In a word, the theory is that the free enterprise market should be encouraged to be as productive as possible – and then the fruits of this productivity should be used, more or less, for social purposes.

It is interesting that social market capitalism claims the loyalty of individuals and groups who come out of a socialist background while also representing the modified views of those who have always been capitalists. The term itself is derived from the programme of the West German Social Democratic Party, which is socialist in origin. That party's 1959 Godesberg Programme outlined various objectives for the social market economy.[2] It represents the dominant approach of the Labour Party in Britain and the social democratic parties of such countries as Sweden, France and Italy. In America, where the descriptive term 'welfare capitalism' is sometimes used instead, most segments of the labour movement and of the Democratic Party are implicitly committed to this ideology – although with poorer conscience, since anything smacking even remotely of socialism is cause for alarm in America. That did not, however, prevent George Meany from stating this kind of philosophy before a Congressional committee in 1959 when asked whether he were a socialist:

> I still do not know what socialism is, despite the things I have read. But if socialism means that under a democratic system, this republican form of government that we have, there are people who desire to secure for the great mass of the people, the workers, the wage earners, the farmers, and others, a better share of whatever wealth the economy produces, and that by providing that better share we provide a broad base of purchasing power to keep the economy moving forward – if that is socialism, then I guess I am a Socialist and have been a Socialist all my life. I do not figure that, but if that is what socialism means, that is the sort of thing I am interested in.[3]

Most of the leading economists in the Western world are supporters of social market capitalism. For our purposes, however, the statement of the case by Oxford economist Denys Munby may be particularly interesting. Munby is a highly competent economist, but he has developed many of his views in writings seeking to relate economic problems to the Christian faith.[4]

Munby defines the 'mixed economy' as one 'in which the state in various ways controls and plans the activities of private business men, and itself engages directly in economic activity as an entrepreneur, but where private business men still play an important role'.[5] Such an economy is desirable 'because it allows for the variety and experiment necessary to human life, and because it sets no rigid and dogmatic bounds to action by the state or private initiative'. By comparison, the dogmas of laissez faire and of collectivism are dangerous.

Munby emphasizes the benefits of the price system ('the only way in which a large scale economic system can satisfy the need of a large population') and its role in allocating resources rationally and in recording the desires of consumers. The price system is not infallible, but it is in an extremely useful way of relating economic needs to available resources so that actual costs can be determined accurately. In this system, the consumer is sovereign. Whenever he chooses among available goods he makes a decision among the different possible uses of resources. Those who oppose this system, therefore, 'should be prepared boldly to admit that they do not believe that consumers should be given this influence'.[6] Sometimes, indeed, they should not. Nevertheless, the presumption should be in favour of using the price system: 'there is an *a priori* case for using it, and there is an even stronger case against interfering with it, unless careful scrutiny is made of the wider consequences of such interference.'[7]

The importance of the price system lends corresponding importance to the social role of the businessman. Besides initiating economic activity, the businessman co-ordinates economic action 'in accordance with the messages that the price system transmits'.[8] The businessman is not to be thought of, therefore, as a greedy parasite. He performs this useful role as middle-man between the consumer on the one hand and productive resources on the other. This is a role which has to be performed in any economic system, and it can be performed particularly well in a system – such as the mixed-economy – where the price system has a degree of autonomy.

But Munby accepts the need for considerable governmental involvement in economic life. Indeed, he argues that nineteenth-century laissez faire was highly unique in economic history. State interference has been far more typical and, on the whole, beneficial. Currently, the mixed-economy state should be prepared to exercise several broad powers. It should be guarantor of law and order. It should establish and maintain the 'rules of the game' by which business activity is governed. It should provide a wide variety of services: military service, police force, town planning, parks, highway system, education, health services, cultural services (including broadcasting and television). It should provide social security. It should manage the economy so as to maintain full employment. It should provide regulation in the economic field, with quality inspection, maintenance of purity of food and safety of medicines, factory safety, construction standards, etc. It should sometimes interfere with the price system – particularly in monopolistic situations. And it should govern interest rates. It should be prepared, in some circumstances, to nationalize industries.

This is quite a list. It goes much further than some would wish, while others would doubtless feel that it does not go far enough. But it provides some idea of how government and the private sector interact in the mixed economy. Summarizing his position, Munby writes that

> If the work done by the private businessman is satisfactory to society, there is no need to interfere, not because we believe that he has any *a priori* natural right to property or profits, but because, if society is functioning aright, it is unwise to interfere. While ills are patent and needing treatment, on the other hand, and there are plenty of them, we do not need to be inhibited from taking action to remedy them because of any theoretical scheme that would propose a policy of non-interference. An empirical approach that ignores the dogmas of the extreme right and left will enable us to use the achievements of the industrial system we have inherited and will also make us ready to experiment more boldly with new forms of collective and community action.[9]

Current writings by advocates of social market capitalism, particularly in Europe, suggest the value of a somewhat more aggressive governmental role. For example, it is suggested by some that government should 'buy into' key industries in order to participate in important business decisions having wider ramifications. Outright government ownership of some competitive businesses can, moreover, serve two very useful purposes. First, it can help provide a quality standard against which private business must then compete (although sometimes this works the other way). Secondly, it can provide government with a vital source of information on the actual costs of production. During the oil crisis of 1973–74, for instance much was made of the fact that governments lacked basic information on the actual costs of locating and exploiting oil resources. Had government been involved more basically in the industry it could better have judged the industry's claims.

These are not unimportant points. They are not, by themselves an argument for full-scale socialization. But they are formidable reasons why government can make the free enterprise system work better by participating in it. Nor can it be argued against such participation that once government 'invades' the business world it will not stop short of collectivizing everything. Here the Western European countries provide a better long-standing model than the United States of how government can participate in business and industry without overwhelming it. In Britain, the governmental television network, the BBC, exists side-by-side with the private and commercial ITV, and both apparently benefit by the competition. In France, Renault is a national industry, while Citroen is not. And so on.

The 'mix' between public and private which is proposed by advocates of social market capitalism is to be determined pragmatically. We may expect it to be somewhat different in every country. The key questions are, how can we make the best use of the benefits of the market? What mixture of public and private will be best for economic life, and how shall we put the wealth produced to best use?

From the standpoint of social justice, the social market approach opens up an interesting possibility: that we can separate the production questions (where efficiency and productivity are important) from the distribution questions (where equality and the meeting of basic human needs are important). Clearly absolute equality would not be feasible in a system depending, as the social market still does to a considerable degree, upon economic incentives. Nevertheless, the social market can certainly do vastly more than laissez faire. At the same time, it provides in principle for the maximization of productivity.

The guaranteed annual income (or negative income tax) proposals in the USA offer an interesting illustration of how far-reaching the social benefits might be without upsetting in the slightest the mechanisms of the market economy. We have already noted that Milton Friedman, who is deeply committed to laissez faire principles, also supports the negative income tax. In one of his few ventures into the, for him, dangerous waters of social market capitalism, Friedman suggests that we can indeed separate the production question from the distribution question – at least up to a certain point. The proposal involves a public provision of a guaranteed minimum level of income to every man, woman, and child, and combines this with certain incentives to continued work on the parts of the recipients. But the important thing is that this benefit is in principle to be given regardless of whether or not the recipients are gainfully employed. If they are, they will then receive more. But if they are not they will still receive the minimum provided by law. The only dispute between Friedman and those who support the social market principle wholeheartedly might be over the size of the basic minimum and whether social benefits should be limited to this basic minimum. Most social market supporters believe that additional benefits in education, medicine, housing, culture, and recreation should similarly be provided. They would insist that there is no *economic* principle that could stand in the way.

From a moral standpoint, the case has much to be said for it. The guaranteed income principle would, in fact, go much further than the social welfare provision of the present Marxist states since in all these income is tied more generally to work. In any case, the social market principle would, at the point of economic distribution, make it possible for society to go a long way toward undergirding the economic well-being and social opportunity of all citizens. Thus, the broader aims of social unity, human equality, and liberation from the unnecessary constraints of nature could well be served. Obviously, much depends upon the political decisions that are made in a social market economy. But the potentiality seems to be there for great advances in the direction of full economic justice.

While listing the theoretical advantages of such a system, we should not overlook the relationship between such an economic order and the health of democratic political institutions. It can be argued that the healthiest democracies today are by and large the countries which have organized economic life along the lines of the social market. This may not be accidental. Unlike the more collectivized systems of the Marxist countries, the mixed economies make it possible for there to be multiple centres of economic power coexisting with government. I shall have more to say on this problem in the following chapter, but it may be noted here that there is a built-in hazard for democracy when all power, economic as well as political, is centralized in the state. That certainly is not a problem with the mixed economy. But unlike the pure laissez faire system, the mixed economies do not in principle deprive the democratic government of the right to exercise power in those economic areas which are of greatest significance to its people. Thus, here too the mixed economy seems to undergird a healthier democracy, at least in principle. Against both collectivism and laissez faire capitalism, it can be argued that the people really 'own' the state more decisively in the Western mixed economy democracies than they do in these other systems. What they *do* with it may be quite another matter. But the possibility exists for them to have the advantages of a great deal of freedom in a market economy while avoiding the disadvantages. So it seems.

The Accomplishments of the Social Market Economies

A cartoonist has provided us with an arresting picture on the cover of a volume dealing with the record of Keynesian economics. In the background there is a graph showing the national unemployment figures and economic fluctuations prior to the publication of Keynes' important book, *The General Theory of Employment, Interest and Money* in 1936, and the vastly improved statistics which have occurred ever since. In the foreground a smug Lord Keynes is depicted smiling benignly at his critics.

Advocates of the mixed economy, such as Paul Samuelson, can well strike the same pose. There is much evidence to be offered in support of their claim that the mixed economy of social market capitalism really does work best in practice. You can't argue with results.

It is certainly true that from World War II until the end of the 1960s, despite a few relatively minor fluctuations, the overall picture of the mixed economies was one of constant economic growth and increased provision of social benefits. Despite the fears of some (including many of the Keynesians), World War II was not followed by a repeat of the Great Depression. Instead, with relatively minor fluctuations in the business cycle, the Western economies boomed ahead. The productive capacities which had been expanded by war production were met by pent up consumer demand based on wartime saving. Western economies, largely managed in accordance with the principles of Keynesian economics, maintained a high growth rate combined with relatively low rates of unemployment and inflation. Some figures may help to make the point. It has been estimated that the Gross National Product per capita in the Western countries increased at the rate of about 2% per year during the century from 1860 to 1960. But the average rate from 1945 on was doubled to about 4% per year.[10] This is the best measurement available to us on the growth of economic production, although it does not tell us about the distribution of goods or the general improvements in well-being. The high US unemployment levels of the Depression (which ranged from 9.9% in 1941 to a high of 24.9% in 1933) levelled off sharply during and after the war. From 1942 to 1971 unemployment never went above 7% and only in the recession year of 1958 was it above 6%.[11] There was some inflation throughout this period, but the rate was relatively low. Measured in constant 1958 dollars, the American Gross National Product increased steadily from $150 billion in 1945 to $741 billion in 1971.[12] These are impressive achievements.

This has also been a period of great inventiveness and of the development of new products for the mass consumer market. One thinks immediately of television, which has swept the world and is now regarded as a virtual household necessity in a number of

Western countries. One thinks of the cheap transistor radio, the development of stereo systems and complex but relatively cheap tape recorders. One thinks of improvements in automobiles and highways (a mixed blessing, to be sure – but quite a productive accomplishment all the same). One thinks of plastics, of frozen foods, of jet planes, of direct distance dialing by telephone, of polaroid cameras, of Xerox copying, of the great revolution in agriculture, of computers, of cheap hand calculators, of open-heart surgery and organ transplants and other incredible improvements in medical technology, of space exploration including visits to the moon, of waste recycling techniques, nuclear energy, and so on and on.

It will immediately occur to most readers that some of these are, like the automobile, a mixed blessing. Some have posed new problems for us concerning pollution, safety, and the conservation of resources – and some raise even the question of human survival. We shall return to this later. But it does need to be registered quite clearly that these immense accomplishments of inventiveness and production are very largely the fruit of economic organization under the mixed economy of social market capitalism. And these consumer benefits do not in themselves begin to convey the further advantages of productive growth in terms of increased worker benefits – not only in real purchasing power but in relation to working hours, vacation time, early retirement, and a lightening of sheer physical labour.

What about the social benefits promised by the theory? Again we can record substantial growth, and not one that is limited to the advanced social welfare programmes of a Sweden or Britain. The projected US Federal budget outlays for fiscal year 1977 included $188 billion for health, labour, welfare and education (including social security) in a total budget of $394 billion. Some of the other budget items, for example in natural resources and environment and in revenue sharing and housing, also reflected welfare-type expenditures. Taken as a whole, the immense variety of programmes and services this represents constituted nearly 10% of the total output of the economy. To this must also be added the expenditures of state and local governments, many of which are for educational and welfare purposes. One could dispute the value of some of the welfare programmes and one could question budgetary choice of priorities – such as the expenditure of nearly $100 billion for defence purposes. But the total volume of such governmental welfare activity is truly impressive.[13]

New Problems in Managing the Mixed Economies

The case for social market capitalism ultimately rests, not upon theory but upon concrete results. The results in the era of Keynes following the Great Depression have truly been impressive. Several years ago it was easy to believe that the problems of inflation and recession – at least in any serious form – were now a thing of the past. The economics of social market capitalism had solved the technical difficulties. We could anticipate continuing economic growth and social benefits until, as Keynes himself expected, ultimately the economic problem itself would be solved.

But after more than a generation of steady and sometimes spectacular success things came unglued. Suddenly in the early 1970s the Western economies were confronting the twin spectres of inflation and recession at the same time. As we have seen, in the first chapter, the standard diagnoses and prescriptions of Keynesian social market economics no longer seemed to fit. What was understood to cure inflation had the effect of aggravating unemployment – without entirely curing inflation either. And what was expected to alleviate unemployment increased inflation – without restoring full employment. Economists dubbed the new situation 'stagflation': a combination of economic stagnation with inflation. What went wrong?

The new problems provided a nice opportunity for the older ideologies once again to parade their wares. Marxists, having faced the discouragements of years of increasing mixed-economy prosperity, could once again speak credibly of industrial crisis and could employ refined versions of their standard analyses. Only the socialist economy could 'work' ultimately. At the other end of the spectrum, advocates of laissez faire blamed the 'stagflation' upon a generation of governmental interference with the economy and called for a return to the pure market economy with a steady increase in money supply as suggested by Friedman. These conflicting pieces of advice were rejected by mixed-economy economists, but no consensus emerged among them as to the real nature of the problem.

One tempting solution in the early '70s was to blame the inflation on the energy crisis which had resulted from the rapid increase in petroleum prices by the newly-formed cartel of oil-producing countries. The increases certainly did boost the price of petrol and the costs of production. But this could hardly account for the inflation since the bulk of the increases came in 1973–74 after the inflation was already well underway. Moreover, it was demonstrated surprisingly by one economist (Professor Richard N. Cooper) that, in balance, the oil price increases had been *deflationary*. The reason for this is that the oil states were not able to spend most of this new income immediately, either on consumer goods or new industrial investment. This vast amount of money was therefore largely withdrawn from aggregate demand or purchasing power and, if anything, should have had the effect of lowering prices a bit! Of course, it could be and was argued in broader terms that the inflation represented a generally greater scarcity of all resources – energy, food, industrial raw materials. According to this argument, we have, in the 1970s, finally had to confront the limits to growth on a finite planet. There is much truth in this, and this helps to account for the combination of inflation and unemployment. Increased scarcity of resources (among the major factors of production) could raise prices by the law of supply and demand. Lack of resources could curtail expansion of production, hence contributing to unemployment. This might be an important part of the problem, particularly if it is also true that some businesses and labour organizations have the power to determine prices and wages largely outside the normal equilibrium of the market system.

This last has been emphasized in one way or another by many economists in the United States and Britain. The problem, as they see it, is no longer simply one of supply and demand. In a world of gigantic producers and immense labour organizations it is now necessary to speak of 'cost-push' inflation. If labour costs are established by wage settlements negotiated between producers and strong unions, then prices will have to reflect the new costs or producers must go out of business. This way of stating it tends to place the onus of inflation upon labour. Actually, the gigantic corporations have proved quite adept at maintaining very large profit margins. Labour costs may be used as justification for raising prices (and profits) even higher than the margin required by increased wages. At any rate, if such market power exists outside the normal supply-and-demand relationships of traditional economic theory, this may have very great importance for our understanding of the new problems.

We should remember that the essence of Keynesian policy was to control the business cycle by managing demand (that is, purchasing power). In a recession, with high unemployment, production could be stimulated by somehow enlarging the purchasing power – usually through governmental spending. In an inflation, purchasing power could be reduced by increases in taxation and by a slow-down in governmental spending. John Kenneth Galbraith and others have noted for some time that it is much easier for government to cope with recession than it is to combat inflation (partly because increased taxation and diminished governmental spending are politically unpalatable). But Galbraith emphasizes that the combined problems of inflation/recession are no longer simply a result of supply and demand relationships.[14] We do not have inflation basically because there is too much purchasing power bidding for the available supply of goods nor do we have unemployment because there is not enough purchasing power to stimulate profitable production. The problem now is that big business is able to control prices at high levels, and big labour is able to negotiate high wages.

In both cases, according to Galbraith, it is because the economic competition assumed by Keynesian economics (as well as by laissez faire capitalist theory) is no longer a dominant factor. According to traditional theory, when prices rise above a certain point, competitors will be attracted into the market, thus bringing prices down again. You could be sure that prices would not be artificially high. Similarly, unemployment could be counted upon to reduce labour costs because the unemployed would be competing (at lower wages) for the jobs of those who refused to work for lower wages. (This might not be competition for exactly the same jobs, of course, but rather going to work at lower wages for competing firms.) The predicted result would be lower wages, lower prices, more sales, more production, more employment. Business competition could be counted upon to keep prices down, supplemented by governmental policies assuring adequate purchasing power to keep business stimulated. Labour competition could be counted upon to assure full employment at market wages under conditions of full production. But the problem now is that we just do not have this competitive situation. Big business and big labour control the markets. Hence prices and profits will continue to rise in spite of lower demand, and wages will remain high in spite of unemployment. In effect, if I understand Galbraith's point correctly, the market power of big business and big labour is capable of holding total production down (but at high profit margins), and some people and productive capacities are simply unused.

If this diagnosis is accurate, then the only feasible solutions would seem to be either a restoration of full-scale competition or some kind of incomes policy. The first alternative, which Galbraith does not really take up, would scarcely seem practicable as a way of increasing total productivity. Small businesses are simply unable to produce on the same scale in a world of highly complex industrial products (although most commentators agree that we do continue to have a highly competitive market in agricultural commodities). It takes too large a concentration of capital to produce automobiles and television sets to expect large numbers of companies to be able to move in and out of production in response to competitive market conditions. In an earlier book[15] Galbraith emphasized that the development of the complex products of industry requires long-range planning and the careful co-ordination of hundreds or thousands of separate processes, often involving long-term contracts with independent suppliers. Planning must include fairly stable prices and built-in profit margins. Vigorous prosecution of the anti-trust laws might help restore some competition, but it cannot correct the basic problem without undermining the advanced state of production. Which leaves only the 'incomes' policy. By this, Galbraith and other economists mean simply a governmental policy establishing the limits to wages, prices, profits, interest rates, and rents – the incomes earned by the various factors of production.

Understandably, governments in the Western world have hesitated before adopting wide-ranging controls of this kind. According to mythology, governmental incomes policies never work. The wartime Office of Price Administration did more harm than good, etc. Galbraith disputes this point, arguing that the OPA was quite effective during World War II in keeping wages and prices in line and that the incomes policy of the first two phases of President Nixon's wage-price freeze beginning in August, 1971 were effective, though incomplete, in controlling inflation and unemployment. Of course the problem remains whether a sufficiently just incomes policy could be devised (covering the literally millions of items) without abandoning the advantages of the market mechanism and without constricting the total output of industry. Would this be a Pandora's box?

The basic problem is underscored by Oxford economist John Hicks' reappraisal of Keynesian economics.[16] Hicks notes that there are two kinds of markets, which he calls 'fixprice' and 'flexprice'. A fixprice market is one in which prices can be and are set by producers. It includes fixed wages established by the wage-push of trade unions having little to do with the law of supply and demand. A flexprice market is one with prices which are still determined by the relationships of supply and demand. The major difference between the two is that 'in the fixprice market . . . actual stocks (of goods) may be greater, or may be less, than desired stocks; in the flexprice market, on the other hand, actual stocks are always equal to desired stocks'.[17] This analysis seems consistent with Galbraith's provided we understand that the market of the great corporations is of the fixprice variety: wages, prices, and profits are determined, not by the simple relationships of supply to demand but by the power of unions and corporations. This power is not unlimited, but neither is it a matter of the market determining prices.

An important contribution of Hicks' analysis is the attempt to understand wage increases in the fixprice situation. If wages do not rise simply as a result of full employment or fall as a result of labour competition when there is a lot of unemployment, how are we to understand the fluctuations? The power of trade unions is important, to be sure; but what determines union goals and demands themselves? Hicks' answer, which may be more significant than he thought, is that it is the general conception of what is a 'fair' wage that ultimately determines the push for wage increases. This is a very complex thing, and it is related to increases in productivity and of the cost of living. But it is also a matter of workers' perceptions of what their wages ought to be compared with the wages (and profits) of others. Thus, a wage-price spiral is not simply a matter of wages pushing to catch up with prices. It is also a matter of workers in one industry trying to 'catch up' with the wage increases of the workers in other industries. This would all be very well if there were generally agreed understandings of what the relative differences of wages should be in different jobs. But, of course, there's the rub!

> What is needed is that the worker himself should feel that he is being treated fairly. In fairness, in that sense, there are many elements; and they do not fit together at all well. It is unfair, says A, that B (whom I think is no more deserving than I am) should get a higher wage than I do; but B, who gets the higher wage, may also think it unfair if A's wage is rising faster than his. C feels it to be unfair if his employer is making large profits, but does not raise his wages; but if he does raise C's wages, others (whose employers are not making such large profits) will think it unfair. It is felt to be unfair if prices are rising and wages are not rising in the same proportion; but it is also felt to be unfair if wages are rising faster than prices, but not so much faster as they did a year or two ago. And so on, and so on. A system of wages which will satisfy all the demands of fairness that may be made upon it is quite unattainable. No system of wages, when it is called in question, will ever be found to be fair.[18]

Non-economists can find this kind of analysis reassuring – both because it obviously conforms to common sense and also because it illustrates how far economists are from having neat, scientific answers! But the problem is still with us. Hicks himself remarks that the thing that keeps some degree of orderliness in the income system is 'the sanction of custom'. We may not all agree on what is 'fair', but there may be broad consensus on what has been *customary*. The governing question is, in effect, what are the 'established differentials' between different jobs? In an inflationary situation, the force of custom embedded in these differentials will keep wages rising even if there is considerable unemployment. The ultimate effect can be to contribute to further inflation and further unemployment.

This situation is obviously something of an embarrassment to the assumptions of social market capitalism. It leads to the question whether in the long haul, this system really is as stable and productive as it is cracked up to be. Keynes himself recognized the difficulties. In his *General Theory* he acknowledged that there could be an intense struggle for higher relative wages among workers – thus leading to the wage-price spiral (or, as Lord Kahn suggests, to the 'wage-wage' spiral).[19] The problem of stagflation is not one that Keynes had to confront personally. But he gave indications of his belief that it is a dangerous policy to attempt to control wages by deliberately creating unemployment (the standard laissez faire 'solution'), and he hoped to find policy alternatives somewhere short of totalitarianism.[20] This is a side of Keynes which received very little emphasis during his lifetime, but the Keynesian mixed-economy economists are having to explore it very seriously today.

The problem, as I see it, is that the key variable has become the political one. It is no longer a matter of objective economic policies to stimulate or constrict demand, thus restoring the full employment-at-low-inflation equalibrium. Now it is more a question of convincing people that they should be satisfied with lower wages or profits than they had hoped for or, alternatively, of finding some way of forcing them to accept lesser wage or price increases. Suddenly we must face political, cultural, and ethical questions head-on. Joan Robinson has remarked that the spiralling wage pressures which have recently contributed so much to inflation are essentially expressions of class struggle. This does not mean that the workers have all suddenly turned to Marxism. It does mean that they are consciously or unconsciously aware of business profit margins. They are increasingly fighting over the distribution of company profit margins.

I do not know the extent to which this is factually true. But the statements by American labour leaders (who are almost to a person anti-Communists) at the time of the Nixonian wage-price freezes and at times of collective bargaining emphasize forcefully the demand for a greater share of the fruits of industry. Whether or not wage increases have in fact kept up with or exceeded productivity may not be important so long as workers and their leaders believe their share is not high enough.

But what is high enough? One is reminded of the celebrated reply made by Samuel Gompers, pioneer leader of the American Federation of Labour. Gompers was asked what labour's ultimate objectives *really* were. His answer was: 'more'. That answer has always been taken to mark the essentially pragmatic style of American labour – a commitment to engage in the give-and-take process of collective bargaining, settling for what can be achieved. But when the 'more' of strong labour combines with the 'more' of powerful corporations, the results may almost surely add up to more inflation and more unemployment.

Lest we leap too quickly to the idea that some other ideological system would prove more capable of dealing with this problem, we should remind ourselves that laissez faire capitalism had to confront the *worst* problems of industrial crisis and depression on a truly massive scale. And we should remember that a Communist or socialist country would have these same workers who, apart from some spiritual conversion to unselfish 'socialist values', would have exactly the same mutually inconsistent ideas of 'fair' wage increases and proper wage differentials. That, in fact, is almost exactly what has led to some problems of stagflation in Yugoslavia, the one Marxist country which has given considerable autonomy to its worker-run industries. Most of the other Marxist countries have solved the problem of wages in a more totalitarian way, which raises its own moral questions.

And so, the social market economy is not perfect by any means, even in doing what it claims to do best. But neither is it in a state of total disarray. From the practical standpoint of sheer economic management much may depend upon the political questions whether a broad new consensus, acceptable to all segments of society, can be devised for the allocation of the fruits of the mixed economy.

Controlling the Multinationals

The problems of managing the mixed economy would be bad enough if we had to be concerned only with economic forces within the nation. But the emergence of multinational corporations on a vast new scale has added further complications along with some intriguing new possibilities. The multinationals are the corporations which may be based in one country but which are deeply involved in producing and marketing their goods in a number of countries. Typically they are great economic empires, with parent companies controlling local subsidiaries. They are often engaged in making and selling a wide diversity of products. Often, as in the case of automobile manufacturers, the final product will be assembled in one country from components manufactured by subsidiaries in several other countries. The multinationals deal in the currencies of many nations and relate themselves in complex ways to the laws of many lands.

Not all of these great corporations are principally based in the United States, of course, but the largest number are. The number includes such well-known names as General Motors, Ford, Standard Oil of New Jersey, ITT, Singer, Xerox, General Electric, US Steel, International Harvester, IBM, and many others. Often such corporations have found their overseas operations more profitable. According to Barnet and Muller, 'about one-third of the total assets of the chemical industry, about 40 percent of the total assets of the consumer-goods industry, about 75 percent of those of the electrical industry, about one-third of the assets of the pharmaceutical industry are now located outside the United States. Of the more than $100 billion invested worldwide by the US petroleum industry, roughly half is to be found beyond American shores.'[21] US corporate experience is similar to that of other industrialized countries, although smaller countries, including Great Britain, West Germany, and France, may proportionately be even more dependent upon such corporations. The far-flung empires of Volkswagen, the Phillips corporation, Royal Dutch Shell, and newer Japanese companies have become highly significant features of world economic life and their home countries are deeply dependent upon them.

Even in a large and powerful country like the United States, it is evident that the multinational corporation poses serious challenges to the nation's management of its own economic life. Fiscal and monetary policies designed to increase production and employment, to raise or lower interest rates, and so on, can be frustrated by the international character of the great corporations. To a large extent these corporations can invest where they choose, open and close plants, hire and fire workers entirely on the basis of their own calculations of profitability. It is more difficult for the social market economy to be orchestrated properly. As British socialist economist Stuart Holland puts it, 'demand orchestration will be ruined as half the orchestra either plays another tune or gets up and leaves the national economic stage'.[22] A country like Britain may be particularly vulnerable. Interestingly, that country is home base for the largest number of the great European multinational corporations, yet its own economic performance has lagged in important respects behind those of West Germany and France. Holland believes this is largely because Britain's own multinationals have chosen to limit expansion in their own country because of the Labour government's economic policies. If so, the point is not whether this is or is not a legitimate reaction to good or bad policies by a particular government. The point is that the corporations have the power to make that decision.

How can these corporations use their power? A couple of illustrations may be helpful. First, they can fight organized labour in the parent country by establishing plants in low-wage countries where unions are either discouraged or forbidden. Americans have noted a vast increase in the number of products and parts of products from such Asian countries as Hong Kong, Taiwan, and South Korea where labour is plentiful and cheap. This is true of clothing, but it is becoming true of more sophisticated products, like cameras and television sets, as well. The process may be similar to the movement of many textile mills out of New England half a century ago in order to establish factories in the cheap labour sections of the South.

The other illustration is one that would not occur to most people, but it is ridiculously simple all the same. It is what some economists call transfer pricing and the international shifting of costs. If a company, say in the United States, is manufacturing goods with component parts produced in several countries, and if it wholly owns the subsidiaries which are producing the components, it is then a fairly simple thing to raise or lower the profit margin either in the parent company or in the subsidiary just by raising or lowering the costs of the component parts. If excess profit taxes are high in the United States, the company can lower its apparent profit by paying a very high price for its components. If taxes are higher in the country where the subsidiary is located, then the same components can be bought from the subsidiary at very low prices. This would lower the subsidiary's profit and raise that of the parent company. Of course, the company can take care to locate important parts of its operations in countries having no taxes at all.

Further complicating matters for the national economic planners, multinational corporations which deal in the currencies of many countries can manipulate their funds in accordance with the most favourable exchange rates. This tends to destabilize the normal exchange of currencies and to frustrate the goals of international monetary arrangements among nations.

We do not need to pursue this point much further. Nor do we need to picture the multinational corporations as evil conspiracies unscrupulously manipulating governments, running roughshod over all their enemies (although it must be admitted that the behaviour of some companies, such as ITT in Chile, can only be called vicious). The public relations departments of any of the multinationals could doubtless bring forth much evidence of their good will and of efforts to accommodate themselves to the interests and sensibilities of the people of the various countries in which they have operations. But the important point remains that these corporations have vast powers which seem to put them beyond the reach of economic life as organized in accordance with the ideology of social market capitalism.

Many of these operations are even beyond the power of nationalization. Barnet and Muller remark whimsically that 'Rumania could, of course, nationalize the plant that makes all the gearboxes for Renault's "Estafette" model, but the gearboxes would sit in Bucharest, since they are useless for any other purpose'.[23] The point is that the multinationals have often gained centralized control of the marketing as well as the manufacture of their products.

Clearly this vast, largely new power of the multinationals is important.

From the broader ethical standpoint we may have to note a certain amount of promise along with the more obvious threat to national sovereignty. But why should national sovereignty be such an important thing ethically? If the rich industrialized countries, led by the United States, enjoyed absolute national sovereignty would this necessarily be a good thing from the standpoint of human justice? Is it necessarily a bad thing that increasing proportions of corporate operations are being set up in the Third World?

Left alone, the rich industrial countries have already shown how unconcerned they can be for the vast and growing disparity of wealth between themselves and the underdeveloped lands. America, which was fairly generous in the immediate post-war period, has provided less and less foreign aid – both in absolute dollar amounts and as a percentage of its gross national product. Prophetic writers, including Barbara Ward and Gunnar Myrdal, have long called upon the industrial countries to devote at least 2% of their annual gross national product to building up the economic potential of the poorer lands, but few have come close to even that fairly paltry sum. In a world containing hundreds of millions if not billions of economically wretched people, can we shed too many tears for the diminished economic sovereignty of the rich?

Critics of the multinationals reply instantly that the power of these vast enterprises is not in any remote way being exercised for the poor of the world. Indeed, a good deal of the production is being directed toward the rich markets and seems designed to increase the dependency of the poorer areas upon the already rich. The point is well taken. Nevertheless, we should understand what it could mean in the long run for vast corporate assets of all kinds to be building up in underdeveloped areas and for the workforce of many of these areas to be increasingly organized industrially. Even Karl Marx would have understood that this could be creating economic realities which the corporate interests will not – in the long run – be able to control. Today the workers of Hong Kong and Taiwan may be working for American industry at dollar-a-day wages. What will happen, ultimately, when they themselves get organized? Is it not obvious that American and European labour unions have the most direct economic stake in making sure they do organize? A multinational giant has great power, but it also has more points of vulnerability than some other companies may have.

That point became clear to me a number of years ago while observing the efforts of Cesar Chavez' Farm Workers' Organization

(FWO) to gain recognition in Florida. Purely local farm operations in Florida were able to withstand the pressure quite successfully. But rather quickly the FWO was able to gain recognition by the Minute Maid Orange Juice Company, a subsidiary of Coca-Cola. Doubtless Coca-Cola could have resisted. But it was vulnerable to all kinds of labour difficulties and consumer boycotts among the farm workers' sympathizers in other states and abroad. Resistance to the farm workers was not considered worth the potential cost.

Translated into international terms, what this means is that the multinationals may be organizing more than their own interests! They could quite unintentionally be forging more of the economic bonds of a world community and contributing ultimately, to a fairer distribution of world economic resources.

I do not wish to describe this as a fact but as a complicating possibility. The fact is that in the short run the multinationals have made life more difficult for the mixed-economy state. This could either lead to more and more problems, or conceivably it could open the way to some long-run solutions.

Before leaving the topic we should acknowledge that some mixed economy writers have been terribly complacent about the relationships involving international capital movements. Thus for instance, the standard liberal text, Samuelson's *Economics* implies that North American investment in underdeveloped regions is simply one more capital transfer with economically reasonable rates of return and with generally beneficient effects upon the labour force of the underdeveloped country, and that nationalization of such enterprise should occur only if the parent (North American) corporation wished to sell. There is no recognition of the host country's right and responsibility to make basic decisions concerning it own fundamental resources. I hope I have misread this meaning of pages 660–62!

Hard Questions for Social Market Capitalism

The mixed economy, thus, leaves us with a mixed impression. At so many points we have to say 'it all depends'. It all depends on how well the social market is in fact managed, on how capable the government is of maintain its independence in the face of economic pressures, on the actual directions of economic productivity and inventiveness in the future, on the political and economic variables of the Third World, on the agreeableness of labour and management. We have not been able to locate decisive reasons for rejecting this ideological frame of reference out of hand. Neither do we have enough reason to say that 'of course' this is the perspective Christians ought to take on economic matters.

A Christian perspective on economic ideology requires us to put some hard questions to those who find this ideology compelling and to those who are its managers. Let me, in summary, suggest what some of these questions might be.

First, *can social market capitalism really get the business cycle under control?* It seemed to do relatively well for a generation or so before things came unglued in the late 1960s and early 1970s. Were those difficulties fairly temporary flaws, or do they point toward deeper, more ominous problems? We shall know, in time; but supporters of social market capitalism must realize that the ideology will be judged on performance here rather than on econometric designs. Performance must surely include really full employment – and not the 4% or so unemployment that American economists and policymakers have been pleased to call full employment, and certainly not the 7.8% unemployment that the Republican administration in the 1970s seemed willing to tolerate. Of course performance also means adequate provision, through jobs or transfer payments, for the increasing economic well-being of the poorest members of society.

Second, *can it deal equitably with the incomes problem without recurrent industrial conflict and deepening social division?* On the face of it, it would seem that the conflict model of Western industrial relations poses problems for Christian moral conscience. Under the circumstances the churches and enlightened citizens generally have been wise in supporting the demand of organized labour for recognition and power. What chance, after all, does one wage-earner have against General Motors? If corporate power is ultimately based upon private profitability, which it certainly is, then labour must have counteracting power. But the question is whether this model of labour relations will ultimately prove ruinous, whether it is a necessary evil, or whether it can lead to greater future harmony and agreed upon shares of industrial income. I do not mean to imply that we are ever likely to develop an economy without conflicting interests, nor should a Christian support a situation in which any persons are powerless to defend their interests. But there is an institutionalization of antagonism in social market capitalism which detracts from mutual commitment to the common good.

Third, *can such a society 'ride the tiger' of great concentrations of wealth successfully over the long haul?* In theory, it is the government that calls the tune. In practice, how can we avoid the overpowering influence of wealth upon government? This is not a rhetorical question with a certain fixed answer. But it is a real question all the same, and it is made all the more real by the vast new powers of the multinational corporation. Perhaps ways can be found for nations working together to bring the multinationals into a structure of accountability. Perhaps international institutions of political economy can be forged to turn these corporations into less ambiguous blessings. Perhaps the ownership of the corporations can itself be devolved more broadly (for example, through union pension funds and/or governmental participation on a wider scale). Whatever the possibilities, we cannot expect the vast concentrations of corporate power to be weakened or shared either automatically or voluntarily. History speaks with one voice on the question whether the wealthy and powerful can be expected to share their wealth and power voluntarily! Perhaps democratic governments can discipline the beast – but they must remember that they are riding a tiger!

Fourth, *can a social market capitalist economy serve as the base for a less greedy society?* Earlier, we took note of the fact that laissez faire capitalism tends to encourage and institutionalize the expression of human greed. Self-centredness becomes a culturally approved attitude toward life. The question remains whether social market capitalism really improves upon this very much. Does not social market capitalism also depend primarily upon greed as the principal motivation for economic endeavour and as a major pyschological leverage in marketing? This problem is more a cultural than an economic one, but this is one of those points where economic systems have implications and effects ranging far beyond the problems of production and distribution.

It may well be that any effective economic system will have to use incentives based upon self-interest and even greed. But capitalistic systems, including the modified social market capitalism, are likely to carry such incentives too far – thus leading to cultural patterns and values which are directly antithetical to Christian faith.

Finally, *can such a form of economic organization lead ultimately to greater economic equality?* I do not think we have the final answer, either way, on this question; but it is a question that has to be pressed very hard by those who believe in the moral presumption for equality. Social market capitalism makes its case for inequality on the basis of its claim that we cannot have adequate production without incentives which ultimately entail inequalities. The claim is that with proper management of the economy, everybody will be so much better off that some inequality will seem a fair price to pay in moral terms. This claim cannot be dismissed out of hand, particularly since no other modern society has succeeded in eliminating inequality either. The trade-off between basic economic security and some inequality may in any event be a good one, if necessary. More would be lost, in moral terms, by insisting upon equality in poverty rather than tolerating inequality in an economy which provided more for everybody. But it is also true that something is lost by inequality. There must be a limit to the overall size of the pie beyond which we cease talking about enlarging everybody's unequal pieces and begin talking about greater equality in the division. The world as a whole hasn't come to that point yet. In Bangladesh and India it is still a question of enlarging the pie; in those countries, and many others, we could not settle for an equal division of present wealth. Relative poverty in a rich land is better than absolute equality in a wretchedly poor one. But, while that observation has present merit in much of the world today, the problem is that it has led to absolute complacency among most supporters of social market capitalism on the final claim of equality.

But that is not true of all such supporters. Lord Keynes himself, the authority *sine qua non* of mixed-economy ideology, anticipated a time when the 'economic problem' would be solved – that is, when economic scarcity would have been overcome. In a world of abundance, humankind could finally give up its preoccupation with money-grubbing economics, and give itself over to more civilized pursuits. In such a world, equality could happen naturally because inequality would no longer matter. When there is an abundance for everybody, then nobody worries about whether he or she is getting enough. You may wish to have more air to breathe or water to drink than I, but I could care less. Perhaps the hippy generation of upper middle class American youths gave us a glimmering of the prospect. On an unacknowledged foundation of almost absolute economic security, these young people were able to live out their liberation from economic concerns. Lower class young people were not taken in by this, but, then they did not have the base of prosperity and we are thinking toward the time when everybody will have that base. It is arguable that that time will never come, since most people – like Samuel Gompers – will always be looking for 'more'. But it is also conceivable that social market capitalism could work its way out in that fashion. Keynes thought it might take about a hundred years, with an annual growth rate of perhaps two per cent. If so, we can be happy that we have been on target for forty years and, having brought the underdeveloped countries into the picture via properly controlled multinational corporations, another two or three generations may see us well on the way toward prosperity and equality for all.

But there are at least two problems with this scenario. One of them is the question of power. Granted we may achieve enough abundance in material goods to satisfy all, will there be enough power to satisfy those for whom that is a ruling passion of life?

Political power, as political theorists remind us, is fundamentally different from economic power. Economic power is expressible in quantitative terms. I have so much, you have so much, and so on. But political power is the power of one *over* the other. So long as there is social organization – i.e., so long as society exists on this earth, political power is likely to be a problem. As we have already said, it needs restraint and accountability. Our problem is that while economic power is not the same thing as political power, it provides important leverage in politics. Even the best visions of Keynesian economics do not take care of this question automatically. The pursuit of wealth for the sake of wealth may, in time, be a fading motive. We may hope so. But then we may still have to reckon with the pursuit of wealth for the sake of the political leverage, the control of human society, which it provides.

The other problem is the question of the relationship between economic institutions and the limited environmental and resource base in the natural world – broadly speaking, the ecology problem. With its striking emphasis upon productivity, social market capitalism seems to presuppose an infinite supply of raw materials and energy sources. But evidence mounts that the world's circuits are, so to speak, becoming dangerously overloaded. Does social market capitalism (or any other existing economic ideology, for that matter) provide us with adequate answers to the essential problem of our living in a finite world?

These, combined with the other hard questions and present inadequacies of social market capitalism, give us reason for also considering the claims of democratic socialism and economic conservationism in the following chapters.

7

The Case for Democratic Socialism

Some North Americans and Europeans who had always thought of socialism as a vast, monolithic, totalitarian movement were treated to a surprise in early 1968. The Czechoslovakian Communist Party, under Alexander Dubcek, launched a democratic reform movement. The idea was stated in the movement's slogan, 'socialism with a human face'. Part of the reform was economic. Inspired by Czech economist Ota Sik, various efforts were to be made to loosen up the system – to decentralize and democratize management, expand trade, and experiment with a price system. So far as ordinary Czech citizens were concerned, however, the most important reforms were aimed at freedom and democratic political reforms. During the 'Prague spring' of 1968 the pent-up soul of Czechoslovakia burst forth with fresh creativity. Literature, drama, political criticism, religious life flourished. A 'Christian-Marxist dialogue' came to the surface, attracting wide public interest. There was some expression of capitalistic sentiment, but by and large the populace seemed committed to building a new democratic socialism, a 'socialism with a human face'.

Before Westerners had much chance to get used to this new phenomenon, however, the invasion by troops from the USSR and other Warsaw Pact countries broke the reform movement and slowly began to reverse the tide toward freedom. Several years later, most of the reforms had been abandoned, and the nation's cultural life was again tightly repressed. The hope of the 'Prague spring' had turned sour, and not many positive things were being said about socialism – either with or without a human face.[1]

Many Americans and Europeans were not surprised by the

Soviet invasion. It was just what they would have expected: the Soviet Union certainly could not have done the socialist cause more damage if it had tried![2] But this reaction by Western critics missed half the point. They overlooked the remarkable fact that a genuinely democratic reform movement had been born in the Communist Party of an Eastern European country. The unhappy fate of the movement proved nothing – for that had been caused from outside. Left by itself, we have every reason to suppose that Czechoslovakia might have succeeded in creating a new brand of democratic socialism. The same kind of thing may, indeed, have taken place in the Chile of Salvador Allende had that popularly elected Marxist government not been 'destabilized' by an intolerant America.[3]

Those who have rejected all socialism out of hand as being undemocratic and those who are opposed to political democracy as being contrary to socialism seem to find it equally difficult to understand democratic socialism. For democratic socialism is based upon the prospect of combining the two.

The Moral Commitments of Democratic Socialism

Democratic socialism in fact has a long history. It has much in common with Marxism, but it has usually sought to emphasize the differences as well as the similarities. It has appeared in different forms in various countries. In America, it is associated with the Socialist Party of Eugene V. Debs and Norman Thomas. In England, it is best known through the Fabian movement of Sidney and Beatrice Webb and George Bernard Shaw. European Social Democratic parties are often more in favour of social market capitalism, but such parties usually include democratic socialists. The socialism of Kenneth Kaunda and Julius Nyerere has emerged as a significant form of democratic socialism in Africa.

Taken as a whole, the movement emphasizes conscience and rationality a good deal more than Marxism. Conscious human choice is considered important: moral values are crucial in determining our choices and our choices influence the course of history. Several basic values are emphasized.

Equality is at the centre of the democratic socialist creed. While different socialists may have different philosophical or religious reasons for believing in equality, it is important to all of them. We may not all be equal in natural endowment, but we are to be considered equal in value. We should therefore be equal before the law and in economic distribution. Most socialists would agree with Condorcet's exclamation: 'De facto equality, the final goal of the social art!'[4] In socialist literature and rhetoric, equality is contrasted with privilege and social hierarchy.

In the ideal socialist commonwealth, equality would not be regarded as painful because people would have given up on the dehumanizing drives of competitiveness. The law of the jungle is uncivilized and dehumanizing. A truly civilized society is based upon co-operation; each person making his or her creative contribution to the betterment of the whole, and each person receiving what he or she needs out of the abundance created by co-operation. The solidarity of the human family replacing the buccaneer individualism of capitalist culture.

Democratic socialists often emphasize that Western capitalist society has become a socio-economic anarchy. The competitive self-seeking of individuals has led to a breakdown of fundamental social purposes. The economy should be directed toward meeting human needs. Instead, it creates unnecessary and harmful wants and neglects many important needs. Those who lack sufficient purchasing power are forced to go without, while those who have too much are able to live wastefully. Trusting in the 'invisible hand', capitalism has placed all of its faith in the accidental and infrequent coincidence of selfish competitiveness and public good. Michael Harrington, who has emphasized this theme in his book *The Accidental Century*[5] believes that this individualistic anarchy has given rise to the literature and art of human disintegration in the twentieth century – the decadence of culture. Society lacks purpose because social purpose is subordinated to disintegrative individual competition. A socialist society, on the other hand, would seek to define its objectives and then to achieve them through rational planning.

Planning would not, however, be done by self-appointed elites. It would be responsible and democratic, not autocratic and paternalistic. People would be free to criticize and to form opposition parties, and important policy-makers would owe their offices to the vote of the people. Within an economy based upon equality, solidarity, and purposeful planning there would no longer be social classes.

William Coats provides us with a good summary of the moral viewpoint of democratic socialism:

> Socialist hope arises out of the agony of Western industrial life. It does not deny the reality of the industrial age: it points to its transformation. It calls for a common life of participation in economic, political, and social destiny. Only in socialism does freedom take on the concrete characteristics of service and communality. Only in socialism is freedom defined in terms of neighborly service and the end to privilege and exploitation.[6]

African Socialism

An interesting variation on the theme is provided by a newly articulate African socialism, whose major spokesmen are President Julius Nyerere of Tanzania and President Kenneth Kaunda of Zambia. The movement may be particularly important as a fresh ideological perspective, since it has authentically African roots. Nyerere in fact remarks that 'the European Socialist cannot think of his socialism without its Father – Capitalism'.[7] African socialism, existed long before any contact with Western capitalism. Nyerere describes the social and moral roots of this tribal socialism:

> The foundation, and the objective, of African Socialism is the Extended Family. The true African Socialist does not look on one class of men as his brethren and another as his natural enemies. ... He rather regards *all* men as his brethren – as members of his ever extending Family....
>
> 'UJAMAA', then, or 'Familyhood', describes our Socialism. It is opposed to Capitalism, which seeks to build a happy society on the basis of the Exploitation of Man by Man; and it is equally opposed to doctrinaire Socialism which seeks to build its happy society on a philosophy of Inevitable Conflict between Man and Man.[8]

Nyerere remarks that 'we, in Africa, have no more need of being 'converted' to socialism than we have of being 'taught' democracy. Both are rooted in our own past ...'.

Nyerere's government in Tanzania has sought to foster a new

birth of African socialism by encouraging the development of communal village agriculture and simple manufacturers, while discouraging the migration of people from the land to overcrowded cities. (There is ground for some optimism concerning the future development of this programme, although much depends upon Nyerere's own charisma and the specifically African setting. It should be noted that the economic base is slender and that the government has been unwilling to tolerate an organized opposition during the period of development.) The future of Tanzania may or may not belong to democratic socialism, but the imagery of the extended family is particularly suggestive and fully in harmony with the values of most democratic socialists.

Economic and Political Analysis

The moral rhetoric of democratic socialism has sometimes led people to dismiss it as unrealistic or utopian. The ideals could be applauded, but mature men and women should be more realistic about the business world. Winston Churchill is supposed to have remarked once that he would be suspicious of the character of any young man who was not strongly attracted by socialism before the age of thirty, but that he would be equally suspicious of the intelligence of any who continued to be socialist thereafter. There has sometimes been a certain vagueness about it. As President of Tanzania, Julius Nyerere has very much been dealing with the real world. But some of his rhetoric might suggest otherwise: (Consider, for example, his comment 'Socialism – like Democracy – is an attitude of mind. In a socialist society it is the socialist attitude of mind, and not the rigid adherence to a standard political pattern, which is needed to ensure that the people care for each other's welfare.')[9] But the image has never been entirely fair. A socialist could say that it is better to be vaguely right than precisely wrong. Nevertheless, democratic socialism has badly needed a foundation of careful economic and political analysis.

It has got it in the recent writings of Michael Harrington.[10] Harrington accepts the basic moral values which have already been discussed. But he also seeks to be realistic about the prospects and possibilities for socialism in the contemporary world. His blade cuts in several directions.

In the first place, unlike many democratic socialists, Harrington seeks to make direct use of Karl Marx and Friedrich Engels. The 'unknown Karl Marx', which Harrington attempts to recover, is the Marx who was basically committed to freedom and democracy. Most of the rhetoric of violent revolution in Marx can, in Harrington's view, be attributed to the unsettling period 1848–50 – and much of Marx's work even during that brief period has been misunderstood. Even the phrase 'the dictatorship of the proletariat' – which the Bolsheviks made so much use of in Russia – had a quite different meaning for Marx and Engels. They were thinking in terms of an advanced industrial country where the proletariat constituted a large majority of the population. They were in effect speaking of government by majority rule – an abolition of minority rule by the bourgeoisie. Even the term 'dictatorship' meant something more like the 'rule' of the state than the connotation of the word which was generally held today. Marx and Engels were, in fact, deeply opposed to 'Blanquism', the doctrine of Auguste Blanqui that a small revolutionary elite should seize control of society and direct it forcibly into the future utopia.

In line with this interpretation of Marx and Engels, Harrington is bitterly critical of virtually every 'Marxist' government in the world. If, he argues pointedly, it matters whether the state owns the means of production, then it matters all the more 'who owns the state'. In the Soviet Union and most other allegedly Marxist countries, the state is in fact owned by a small bureaucratic elite. The people are every bit as alienated from the productive process and from the state in such a society as they are in socialism at all.

> The people can own the state in only one way: through the fullest and freest right to change its policies and personnel. Therefore in a nationalized economy exclusion from political power is not something unfortunate that happens in a 'superstructure'; it determines the social and economic base of the system itself, it secures class power to those who 'own' the state, which owns the means of production.[11]

Nor does Harrington consider it to be an accident that Soviet Communism functions undemocratically.

> Under communism, it is precisely the totalitarian monopoly of political power that allows the bureaucracy to extract the surplus

> from the direct producers and use it for its own ends. If the producers were allowed to participate in those decisions, it would signal a revolutionary shift of control from the top to the bottom. For then the bureaucracy could retain its position in society only if the masses voluntarily voted to tax themselves in order to build even more steel mills and better apartments for the party hierarchy and to finance the secret police.[12]

Harrington is particularly bitter about Soviet totalitarianism because it has led so many people to think of socialism as a whole in these terms.

But then comes the question: What has gone wrong in totalitarian Communist societies?

According to Harrington the problem is that a very important Marxist truth has been ignored. The truth is that you cannot socialize poverty. Socialism depends upon the prior achievement of abundance. Lenin, and many subsequent Communists, believed that it would be possible to 'skip stages' in the historical process, with the 'vanguard of the proletariat' leading the society through the stage of industrial development and into socialism. What actually has happened is that socialists have had to bear the brunt of forced savings in order to accumulate the capital for industrial development. And their rule has become fixed and hardened by the privileged self-interest of the new ruling class.

Harrington is therefore profoundly sceptical of the socialist pretensions of most of the 'socialist' countries, and he is pessimistic about efforts of countries in Africa and Asia to move directly toward socialism. You cannot socialize poverty. Where there is scarcity, there will be the objective basis for conflicts of interest. Realistic socialists will join in the struggle to create that abundance and, in the wealthy countries of Europe, North America, etc., they will seek to achieve the socialism for which an objective basis already exists. (Of all the Marxist countries, interestingly, Czechoslovakia had perhaps the most adequate basis for abundance and socialism, and here democratic socialism first seemed possible.)

As for the transition to socialism in countries like the United States, Harrington is convinced that the proletariat (i.e., industrial workers) truly hold the key. It cannot be the urban poor and other marginal members of society. Only labour has the political potentiality of effective social transformation. Nor does organized labour impress Harrington as being as reactionary as many believe. There is a long socialist tradition in the labour movement which has not been recognized because it has reacted so strongly against the socialist label. The unions have, in his opinion, in effect created a social democratic party within the Democratic Party. This is the force which can realistically be expected to further the evolution toward socialism in America.

Harrington supports most liberal reformist measures on the grounds that, while incomplete, they point in the right direction. He does not believe that real socialism can be created overnight. It certainly cannot be imposed upon people who neither understand nor accept it. But several next steps may become realistic. For one thing, as many of the necessities of life as possible (medicine, housing, transportation, adequate nutrition) should be made free – that is, their costs should be borne by society collectively. 'The change in moral atmosphere such a new mode of distribution would portend would be profound.'[13] This would be an important step in the direction of distinguishing between economic needs and economic luxuries, and it would lead away from the tendency in capitalist society for people to sacrifice needs for luxuries.

Further moves could include a reform of inheritance tax laws. He suggests 'providing for relatively low death duties on the first transfer from father to son, which would encourage the father, and very high rates on the second transfer, from son to grandson, which would give the son a reason to strive as hard as his father'.[14] Government should increasingly participate in the control of investments. A governmental investment fund could be made the recipient of steep inheritance taxes, there could be governmental majority participation on corporate boards, and more out-and-out public corporations (on the model of the Tennessee Valley Authority) could be created. The tax policies of a socialist reform programme should aim, not just at income but at *wealth*.

Lest this should all seem to reflect only a self-centred American nationalism, Harrington calls for a restructuring of the world market with major efforts on the part of advanced industrial countries to include the underdeveloped lands in an increasingly prosperous world. At the very least, workers in the more wealthy countries now need to be concerned about labour conditions and wages abroad. Efforts to organize the foreign workers who are presently being exploited by the multinational corporations in underdeveloped countries will benefit both the workers in the parent industrialized country and the foreign workers themselves.

Harrington's views are largely shared by the British democratic socialist Stuart Holland, although Holland's emphasis is upon the need to gain control over what he calls the 'commanding heights' of the economy. Holland speaks of the new 'mesoeconomic' sphere ('meso' meaning middle – between microeconomic and macroeconomic spheres). The mesoeconomic sphere is that of the giant multinational corporations whose power dominates the present scene, frustrating efforts by mixed-economy governments to control macroeconomic policy. Holland believes that only socialism will finally control the mesoeconomic corporations. Like Harrington, he suggests concrete moves to involve government in the control of these corporations. He believes that substantial control might be gained through nationalization of a handful of the largest corporations. The decisions of these government-controlled corporations would affect all the rest, and government would in any case gain much more accurate information on actual costs and trends in the mesoeconomic sphere. Like Harrington, Holland is totally committed to democratic politics. He considers the Labour Party in Britain to be the promising vehicle for future change, and his advice is largely directed toward that party and its natural supporters.[15]

Through writers like Harrington and Holland, democratic socialism has gained careful economic and political analysis without losing its basic moral commitments.

The Claim of Christian Socialism

Once, following a lecture to students, Paul Tillich was asked whether he still supported socialism. The eminent theologian's answer came quickly: 'That is the only possible economic system from the Christian point of view.' This exchange took place in 1957. Years earlier, Tillich had been one of the leaders of the German movement for religious socialism. After being forced out of Germany during the Nazi period, Tillich re-established an academic career in the United States. Most of his writings dealt with systematic theology and the relationship between theology and psychology and the arts. Only rarely did he speak on socialism. But it is of interest in the history of twentieth-century theology that this early commitment to socialism never lost its hold on the thinking of one of the great theologians of this century.

We may take this as symbolic of the persistence of socialism in some Christian circles going back at least to the Christian socialism movement in mid-nineteenth-century England. The movement had considerable vitality then, as it also did during the American 'social gospel' period around the turn of the century. And it has taken a new lease on life today, especially among Christians of the Third World, but by no means restricted to them.[16] It has never been a very carefully defined movement (there is in fact some question as to just how 'socialist' the mid-Victorian Christian socialists really were). But the ideological commitments of the movement have usually been to democratic socialism as we have been discussing it. It has been against selfish economic competitiveness, against the profit motive, against inequality. Often, but not always, it has rejected Marxism. It has been in favour of economic co-operation based upon the solidarity of the human family. While reposing great faith in the goodness of humanity, the movement has often (particularly with thinkers like Walter Rauschenbusch) tried to be realistic about the selfish tendencies in human nature. Such realism has, in fact, served to support the commitment to socialism. Socialism is an important institutional control upon self-seeking. Rauschenbusch was partly thinking of the need for more socialistic economic institutions when he remarked that a 'Christianized' social order would be one where bad people would be required to do good things – just as the present capitalistic order compels good people to do bad things.

The question we must now face is a simple one. Is there not an open and shut case for democratic socialism from the Christian standpoint? How could Christians support any other economic ideology?

We must recall the basic moral values introduced in Chapter 3: The basic Christian commitment to love, to a conception of our fellow humanity, our being one family in God. The serious regard for the material well-being of every member of this universal human family. The belief in equality before God, and its implications for equality of treatment in society. The regard for individual self-expression and freedom. The recognition of the power of human sinfulness. Do not all of these perspectives lead more or less directly to some form or other of democratic socialism? Mustn't we agree, finally, with Tillich on this?[17]

This book will not work its way around to a disagreement with that judgment. There *is* a certain *prima facie* case to be made for the claims of a Christian democratic socialism. It seems to move *directly* to the accomplishment of the Christian's major economic objectives, where the various forms of capitalism must rely upon the indirect visitations of the 'invisible hand' to do what ought to be done. It embodies a prophetic judgment upon the injustices and evils of capitalism – the encouragement of selfishness, the perpetuation of poverty, the continuation of class conflict, the wastefulness, the concentration of vast economic powers in a few hands and, with it, the great strain placed upon genuine democracy.

Blind Spots in Democratic Socialism?

Still, the ideology of democratic socialism also is vulnerable to certain blind spots which may lead us to hesitate before endorsing it without reservation. We must take up some of these troublesome points.

There is, first, the problem of sheer productivity. We do not need to make a god of this, as capitalists often do, to recognize its importance in the ethical scheme of things. The right kind of productivity is essential to humankind's progressive liberation from undesirable limitations of nature. Food, clothing, shelter, transportation, communication, medical care, recreation, even the control of waste and pollution, depend finally upon the right kind of productivity. Most socialists are well aware of this and some socialists may even stress it too much (a matter we shall return to in the next chapter). But the question is whether there may not be some unrecognized elements in the democratic socialist scheme of things which would inhibit productivity or at least not encourage it enough. History has already relegated von Mises' unrestrained claims in this regard to the rubbish heap (' . . . the failure of all 'experiments' with nationalized business in the Western countries. . . the undisputed fact that the average standard of living is incomparably higher in the capitalistic countries than in the communist countries'[18]). But it is not yet clear that we can do as well without the market mechanism, and there is the further question whether a worker-controlled state would democratically agree to devote enough production to capital goods industries rather than consumer goods. The Soviet Union has put too much into capital goods, but the Soviet Union is not democratic. There is the related question whether workers would accept the introduction of more efficient machinery that might mean loss of jobs.

Speaking to this point, Stuart Holland acknowledges that 'majority workers' control in individual companies would act as an obstacle to rationalization and modernization unless society as a whole, through democratized planning structure, has the means to provide guaranteed jobs and income in rewarding work to those who would otherwise lose by rationalization.'[19] To do this, the alternative jobs would have to be as rewarding and convenient, and this then raises again the question whether such a socialist state could really build in a market pricing mechanism that would translate consumer desires into production priorities and effective cost accounting while at the same time not interfering with the broader priorities of society as a whole. The problem is not unique to socialism, and it may be solvable in a socialist context. But, if so, it will take a good deal of creative imagination.

A related question is whether democratic socialism can make provision for genuine economic creativity. One does not have to believe in cut-throat competition to see the importance of this question, and socialist rhetoric certainly emphasizes the importance of creativity. But if the hallmark of socialism is social ownership of the means of production, then a certain dilemma cannot be avoided. If social ownership means ownership and control by the central government (which may itself be controlled democratically), then there is likely to be a vastness of scale which might inhibit really free creativity. How many layers of bureaucracy would one have to go through to pursue a new idea? Where would one get the resources, apart from high-level decisions? On the other hand, if economic life is decentralized along guild socialism lines (as suggested by contemporary Yugoslavian practice), how are we to avoid the emergence of further competition and inequalities? The problem may not be inherently beyond solution. The great creativity which has been forthcoming in the civil service of mixed-economy countries may be suggestive. But this is not the kind of problem we can count upon to solve itself.

This points to the wider problem of concentration of power. Most of the current socialist countries are not exactly reassuring in this respect. To be sure, Bolshevik socialism cannot be confused with democratic socialism, and we must not therefore saddle the latter with responsibility for undemocratic practices in the USSR, North Korea, Albania and other places. But even African socialism is not yet able to deal with the concentration of power problem in a fully democratic way, despite its great promise in other respects. Can there be, in a democratic socialist state, sufficiently independent centres of power to protect us against bureaucratic stuffiness in the present and the possibility of outright tyranny in the future? Will there be enough checks and balances?

We should remember that the problem of concentration of power is not limited to the question whether a few power-seeking individuals will find it possible to seize control of a society's destiny. It could come about that a great concentration of power would permit a number of powerful interest groups to dominate the rest of society. As in the matter of all civil rights questions, the issue is what happens to the minority. What opportunities are available to people who are regarded as mistaken, irrelevant, or bothersome by their more powerful fellows?

The democratic socialist tradition has resources for dealing with this – not least in a typical concern for civil liberties. But it needs to bring that concern more sharply to focus upon the prospect of a much more centralized concentration of political and economic power in almost any imaginable socialist state. One very concrete question it must ask is how it would assure the existence of a free and independently critical press. More than censorship is involved here. It is a question of where, in a socialistically centralized society, the media of communication would find material resources with which to operate without political interference.[20]

Finally, we should repeat that there is a potential blind spot over nationalism. The moral values espoused by most democratic socialists are truly universal. But the institutional frame of reference for the politics of democratic socialism is national. What is there to guarantee that a perfectly socialist nation state would not be utterly selfish in its relationships to the rest of the world? It is, at least theoretically, quite possible for socialist countries to exploit underdeveloped countries as much as capitalists do. A socialist country, quite as much as a capitalist one, can seek to maintain unfair trade relationships. It can be quite imperialistic. Some socialist writers, including Stuart Holland, emphasize that the multinational corporations undermine the self-determination – the national sovereignty – of countries. Holland offers this as another reason for supporting socialism. Yet national sovereignty, by itself, is potentially a very selfish moral cause.

Socialism does not necessarily lead in this direction, of course, But it would be a serious blind spot for socialists to believe that socialism for the nation means justice for the world. It may or may not mean a greater tendency toward concern for the rest of the world. As a matter of fact, I believe that the more equality and less division there is within a nation, the more likely it is that its people will be receptive to the needs of others. But self-centred complacency is also a conceivable result. It is at least possible, over the long run, that the multinationals will lead to a more universal justice. I do not really think so; but it is at least possible. My main point is that those socialists who do not recognize the best possibilities in social market capitalism and the worst possibilities in democratic socialism are likely to approach both ideological tendencies with dangerous blind spots before their eyes.

At one point, both the social market capitalists and the democratic socialists may indeed have the same blind spot. That is in their attitude toward the limitations imposed by nature itself. In recent years, the problem of ecology – with its many ramifications touching upon energy and resource depletion and pollution of the environment – has caused many thoughtful people to lose faith in all of the old ideologies and to seek to forge a new one based upon a new respect for the natural processes and limits of planet earth. To this new ideological tendency we must now turn.

8

The Case for Economic Conservationism

> It must always have been seen, more or less distinctly, by political economists, that the increase in wealth is not boundless: that at the end of what they term the progressive state lies the stationary state, that all progress in wealth is but a postponement of this, and that each step in advance is an approach to it...
>
> John Stuart Mill (1857)

Each of the four economic ideologies we have examined has a notable history. The present debate is not completely new, of course. But it has overtones which have echoed and re-echoed for many years. The four ideologies have also represented answers to many of the same questions, however much the answers may differ. These answers have encompassed the distribution of wealth, the stimulation of production, the control of the economic process, the issues of employment and trade and capital accumulation and government planning versus the free market. Each has had to account for inflation and recession.

A relatively new movement now asks us whether these are really the important questions after all. This movement, which is beginning to gain significant ideological expression, was anticipated by John Stuart Mill's conception of a 'stationary state'. It is based upon growing alarm over the results of rapid industrial expansion in the modern world. It is concerned about the vast and seemingly unavoidable destruction of the natural environment and the wasteful depletion of non-renewable resources. It notes the alarming rate of population growth and the increasing difficulty of feeding the world's people. The ideology of this movement can be summarized in a sentence: *Unlimited economic growth is not possible in a finite world.* Our basic economic posture cannot therefore be expansionist. Neither capitalist expansionism nor socialist expansionism is pointed in the right direction, for neither has caught the main lesson a finite world has to teach us. That lesson is that we must come to terms with nature and develop our economic life in harmony with the limited and limiting natural forces. The ideology can be called economic conservationism if we mean by this that its main focus is upon conserving limited resources and conserving the human values that are threatened by a single-minded concentration upon more and more production. The conservationist theme is evident also in the concern for future generations yet unborn – conserving the future prospects of human life on this planet. Economic conservationism thus seeks to illuminate a crucial choice confronting the late-twentieth-century world: Either we must drastically limit our production and consumption for the sake of an unlimited human future or we shall have a limited future for the sake of unlimited present economic activity.

The Factual Situation

The appeal of economic conservationism depends largely upon one's diagnosis of the factual situation. From that standpoint, there is no question but that the rapid increase of environmental pollution (air, lakes, streams, etc.) and the world's sudden confrontation with a petroleum shortage in the 1970s have had a great impact upon world opinion. Such things can be explained away. It can be said that pollution is controllable, not by limiting production but by directing it more effectively, by developing new energy sources (including solar power), and by inventing and producing more anti-pollution devices and processes. Present shortages can be explained in terms of political and economic forces, such as the Middle Eastern conflict. It can be argued that there is enough food to go round if we would distribute it more justly. And so on.

Such optimistic appraisals should not be dismissed without rigorous examination. But even the more optimistic among us are increasingly willing to admit the crucial points: We do live on a finite planet, the 'spaceship earth'. Some of the resources upon which we depend most, including the fossil fuels, are indeed non-renewable and limited. The atmosphere and water supplies of the planet are both limited and vulnerable to contamination, and environmental pollution has reached dangerous proportions in recent years. We have long since proved our ability to poison fish and drive whole species of animals and birds to extinction. We are thoroughly capable of befouling the environment and undermining the future health and economic well-being of generations yet unborn. The population explosion, whether or not it has yet reached crisis proportions, could well create vast wretchedness and starvation even in our own time – and it certainly will do so eventually if it is not checked soon enough. Such points are increasingly accepted by reasonable people, although opinions vary as to how far things have gone and how much time we still have to correct them and whether desperate emergency measures are called for now.

In short, there is enough cause for concern in the objective situation to suggest the need for a new ideological perspective, and the economic conservationists are beginning to respond. A variety of emphases – some of them mutually incompatible – are emerging in their writings. All seem to agree concerning the central proposition, however: Unlimited economic growth is not possible in a finite world. Since all of the industrialized countries, capitalist and socialist alike, are expansionist and production-oriented, the economic conservationists find themselves unable to endorse either of these ideological systems wholeheartedly.

The American economist Kenneth E. Boulding gave important impetus to this new perspective with his 1966 essay 'The Economics of the Coming Spaceship Earth'. Thinking of the earth as a spaceship, Boulding noted that on a spaceship a premium must be placed upon conservation of all resources for life support. In economic terminology, 'output' cannot exceed 'input' over the long run. We are currently using the 'input' of billions of years of stored-up fossil fuel resources much faster than these can be replenished by the sun and the growth and decay of vegetation. Our actual use of resources should be slowed down dramatically and the products we use should be designed for maximum durability: 'In the spaceman economy, what we are primarily concerned with is stock maintenance, and any technological change which results in the maintenance of a given stock with a lessened throughput (that is, less production and consumption) is clearly a gain.'

Three other recent spokesmen for economic conservationism can be singled out for particular notice.

E. F. Schumacher: 'Small is Beautiful'

The British economist, E. F. Schumacher, has attracted wide attention with his 1973 volume, *Small is Beautiful: A Study of Economics as if People Mattered*.[1] Schumacher's thesis is both technical and moral. On the technical level, he is impressed by the inability of normal economic analysis to comprehend the environmental problem: 'economic growth, which viewed from the point of view of economics, physics, chemistry and technology, has no discernible limit, must necessarily run into decisive bottlenecks when viewed from the point of view of the environmental sciences.'[2] The problem can be explained in economic terms by reference to the distinction between capital and current income. No business would consider itself healthy if it had to balance its books by consuming its capital. But that is exactly what industry as a whole is doing by rapidly consuming the non-renewable resources which took nature billions of years to create. These non-renewable resources, particularly the fossil fuels, appear on the cost-accounting ledgers in exactly the same way as such renewable raw materials as agricultural products and human labour power. Thus, industry has 'the illusion of unlimited powers'.[3] We believe we have solved the age-old problem of production, but our production is based upon diminishing resources and borrowed time.

The moral aspect of Schumacher's thesis is equally compelling. It is that we have allowed ourselves to become increasingly driven by the gods of productivity and consumption, substituting the empty life of materialism for the fuller possibilities of human creativity and culture.

> If human vices such as greed and envy are systematically cultivated, the inevitable result is nothing less than a collapse of intelligence. A man driven by greed or envy loses the power of seeing

> things as they really are, of seeing things in their roundness and wholeness, and his very successes become failures. If whole societies become infected by these vices, they may indeed achieve astonishing things but they become increasingly incapable of solving the most elementary problems of everyday existence. The Gross National Product may rise rapidly: as measured by statisticians but not as experienced by actual people, who find themselves oppressed by increasing frustration, alienation, insecurity, and so forth.[4]

There is, he reminds us, 'a revolutionary saying that "Man shall not live by bread alone but by every word of God".'

This theme, as the words themselves suggest, has important rootage in the Hebrew-Christian religious tradition. But it is interesting that Schumacher chooses to appeal for support from the Buddhist faith. Buddhist economics has, in his judgment, much to teach the West concerning the function of work. It is 'to give a man a chance to utilise and develop his faculties; to enable him to overcome his egocentredness by joining with other people in a common task; and to bring forth the goods and services needed for a becoming existence'.[5] The purpose of work is not to create leisure, and the purpose of leisure is not to avoid work. Rather, work and leisure belong to each other in the rhythms of a fulfilled human existence. Thus, also, the Buddhist point of view does not see *maximum* consumption as ideal, but rather *optimal* consumption: 'the aim should be to obtain the maximum of well-being with the minimum of consumption.'[6] We should plot a 'Middle Way' between the false extremes of growth and stagnation.

Schumacher does not, however, call for the abandonment of all economic growth. He has not exactly proposed a back-to-the-spinning-wheel technology, although he does seek an 'intermediate technology' on a more human scale based upon a lower average cost of development for each 'workplace'.[7] The result would be a much more labour-intensive and a much less capital-intensive technology. In the industrialized countries, this could mean a deliberate slowing of the pace of economic expansion and productivity, although there would always be need for invention and growth. There will be a continuing need to devise new ways to solve economic problems within the limits of an intermediate technology.

An intermediate technology would also be based upon full employment. In the underdeveloped countries, this would force a new definition of the development task. Whereas current development strategies seek to bring the less developed countries 'up-to-date' technologically as soon as possible, the higher priority of intermediate technology is to put everybody to work. In many such countries large numbers of people for whom agriculture no longer provides a livelihood cannot find industrial work either since industry has sought to use the latest available labour-saving technologies. Hence, despite the enormous economic needs, the labour-power of millions of people is wastefully neglected. An intermediate technology would train such people to make their own tools and then use them to advance the rate of development of their countries: 'If there is a political ideology that sees development as being about people, then one can immediately employ the ingenuity of hundreds of millions of people. . . .'[8] Schumacher therefore stresses education as the primary development task.

In a brief discussion of current economic ideologies, Schumacher manifests a good deal of sympathy for the socialist position. At the same time, however, his own perspective clearly transcends traditional socialism. Much depends upon the cultural values of the society. If those values are based upon materialism and self-seeking, then the society cannot benefit particularly from socialism: 'A society ruled primarily by the idolatry of *enrichissez-vous*, which celebrates millionaires as its culture heroes, can gain nothing from socialisation that could not also be gained without it.'[9] Private enterprise, operating with 'terrifying simplicity' has already demonstrated its immense productivity. If productivity is to continue to be our absolute preoccupation, then a shift to socialism cannot be expected to raise it particularly, even though it may not lower it either. 'There is therefore really no strong case for public ownership if the objectives to be pursued by nationalised industry are to be just as narrow, just as limited as those of capitalist production: profitability and nothing else.'[10]

Schumacher consciously aims this point at the British debate over nationalization, but it may be equally relevant in many of the Marxist countries where virtually everything is nationalized in one way or another. In all such places the danger is that socialism will simply mean a way of organizing life around economic ends, when the real problem is how to organize economics around broader human values.

> What is at stake is not economics but culture; not the standard of living but the quality of life. Economics and the standard of living can just as well be looked after by a capitalist system, moderated a bit by planning and redistributive taxation. But culture and generally, the quality of life, can now only be debased by such a system.[11]

Schumacher's attitude toward socialism remains clouded by his realization that that ideology can lead into the same trap. Moreover, he continues to regard private ownership of small-scale enterprises as 'natural, fruitful, and just', while believing nationalization of larger-scale enterprises to be desirable.

Thus, Schumacher cannot be described adequately either in terms of social market capitalism or democratic socialism. Critical of both, he points us toward an enlarged ideological perspective in which economics is subordinated to human considerations and in which we have learned to live within the limitations of our nature and the physical world.

Herman E. Daly: The Steady-State Economy

On the American side of the Atlantic, economist Herman E. Daly is among a small but increasing number of intellectuals who believe that the limited nature of the physical world should begin to dominate economic ideology. Daly bases his views to a large extent on scientific distinctions between 'low entropy' and 'high entropy' states of raw materials and energy. Matter and energy, according to the laws of thermodynamics, can neither be created nor destroyed. But they can be relatively more accessible or less accessible for productive use. Low entropy means that they are relatively accessible; high entropy that they are not. For instance, a gold mine might represent low entropy of the precious metal since it could be mined with relatively little expenditure of energy. But a pound of gold dust scattered from an aircraft at 40,000 feet would create a very high entropy. The pound of gold would continue to exist. But it could never be brought together again. Similarly, a vast deposit of petroleum not far below the surface of the earth represents low entropy, because it is in fairly accessible form, while the oil locked up in the shale rock of Colorado and Canada has a much higher entropy. Humpty Dumpty sitting on his wall has low entropy. After his fall, he has very high entropy, all the king's horses and all the king's men being unable to put him back together again.[12]

We are currently using energy and material resources which nature, through billions of years, has placed at our disposal in a reasonably low entropy state. We do not destroy these resources, in one sense, because neither matter nor energy can be created nor destroyed. But we turn them into a high entropy state. As matter and energy sources of low entropy are used up, it takes increasingly larger amounts of energy to make them usable. The case of fossil fuels is a particularly crucial illustration. It took nature billions of years to store the petroleum, natural gas, and coal which have fuelled the industrial revolution. But these resources, however vast, are finite. Once they are gone, they will be gone forever. Even mineral resources, such as iron and copper and tungsten, are being taken from low entropy states and dispersed as high entropy.

Our problem, then, is to live within our entropic limits. Daly believes that in the long run we shall have to settle for a 'steady-state' economy, which means that we must minimize the use of irreplaceable low-entropy sources of energy and matter, that we must maximize the durability of the goods we produce, and that we must minimize the dispersal of waste material. Thinking of the economy as a vast input-output system, the input must be small and the throughput must be slow in order that the output will also be low. Input here refers to the rate at which we claim and use raw materials and energy; throughput refers to the rate at which things are consumed or used up; and output refers to the discard of waste. When waste is recycled, the effect is to lower the net input in the system. Over the long run, we must be able to sustain economic life on the basis of renewable or recyclable sources of matter and energy (solar heat is a good illustration of the latter). Otherwise, there will literally be no future for the human race. Recent calculations that it cost nature approximately $1 million to produce every gallon of petroleum over the eons helps to dramatize Daly's point. If we were forced to pay even one hundredth of a per cent of that (which would be $100) per gallon of petrol for our cars, the point would be quite clear indeed. Yet, we are in fact paying more than that if we consider the human future realistically. Put in another way, Nicholas Georgescu-Roegen reminds us that 'every time we produce a Cadillac, we irrevocably destroy an amount of low entropy that could otherwise be used for producing a plow or a spade'[13] (or, actually, many plows and spades).

Our problem is that present economic systems are based upon the goal of increasing production, whereas our need is to decrease production as quickly as we can without undermining the health and safety of existing human beings until we have arrived at a steady-state economic balance. Daly defines this point 'as an economy in which the total population and the total stock of physical wealth are maintained constant at some desired levels by a "minimal" rate of maintenance throughput (i.e., by birth and death rates that are equal at the lowest feasible level, and by physical production and consumption rates that are equal at the lowest feasible level)'.[14] Like Schumacher, Daly's vision calls for continuing inventiveness and economic progress. But physical wealth and population as a whole must finally arrive at a plateau in a finite world.

Turning to other problems addressed by more traditional economic ideologies, Daly points out that our 'growthmania' has made it easy for us to evade responsibility for inequality and underemployment. Inequality could be tolerated so long as everybody's share of the pie continued to grow. And economic growth has made it possible for us to continue to link income to jobs, while insisting that employment be defined more or less in relation to the production process. In a steady-state economy, these escapes will not be possible, and we shall have to confront the demand for equality of consumption and for fulfilling employment opportunities in more radical form. This would seem to point in some kind of socialist direction, but Daly (like Schumacher) also notes that 'socialist states are as badly afflicted with growthmania as capitalist states. The Marxist eschatology of the classless society is based on the premise of complete abundance; consequently, economic growth is exceedingly important in socialist theory and practice.'[15] But Daly, also like Schumacher, obviously believes that neither socialism nor capitalism, with their present assumptions, is capable of handling the main issue – which is that we must subordinate economic systems to the given 'biophysical system of ecological interdependence'.[16] Both capitalism and socialism are infected by growthmania. Political economy must therefore go beyond if we are to achieve a steady-state economy and at the same time structure a peaceful and just society.

At one point Daly's ideological viewpoint presents a contrast with Schumacher's. While Schumacher emphasizes the economic and moral importance of work, Daly wishes to stress the value of leisure. The payoff for growth in productive efficiency should be more meaningful leisure, not more products. His proposed 'strategy of leisure-only growth' does not require material inputs and thus is consistent with the maintenance of the steady-state equilibrium.[17]

Robert L. Stivers: The Sustainable Society

The main thrust of Daly's conception of a steady-state economy is reflected in Robert L. Stivers' vision of a 'sustainable society'.[18] Stivers, who writes from an explicitly Christian ethical background, has borrowed the term 'sustainable society' from a conference of the World Council of Churches. Generally, it means a society whose patterns of economic, political, and social life can be sustained for an indefinite future. Stivers prefers this term to the more narrowly economic terminology of 'steady-state economy' or 'equilibrium economy' because it better conveys the broader dimensions of social reorientation that the world must now undertake.

In economic terms, the sustainable society 'would be an economy in which population and annual product would be (1) sustainable indefinitely without sudden and uncontrollable collapse and (2) capable of meeting the basic material needs of *all* people. Such an economy would necessarily be in equilibrium with basic ecological support systems and would minimize, not maximize, the consumption of nonrenewable resources.'[19] Growth would not be eliminated. But growth would be 'differentiated'. It would eliminate environmentally unsound forms of growth, and it would be concerned with human welfare. The costs of reordering will be considerable, including changes in incentive systems, a revamping of transportation, less energy consumption, changes in suburban living patterns, and so on.

In political terms, the sustainable society will require institutions more capable of distributing the more constant stock of economic goods more equitably. Quarrelling a bit with Schumacher, Stivers reminds us that total decentralization of political institutions would undermine the prospects for global redistribution. Some forms of decentralization may be necessary. But we should note some political drawbacks as well: 'It is potentially anarchic. It is vulnerable to exploitation by individual units. It cannot ensure that all small units will pursue an equilibrium policy. It encourages an uneven distribution of the world's resources.'[20] Total decentralization overlooks the degree to which natural resources are unevenly distributed. At the same time, total centralization of world political and economic institutions is potentially very dangerous – suggesting the world of Orwell's 1984. Stivers therefore advocates 'some kind of mix' – a combination of globally oriented authority 'to manage a worldwide sustainable society, to ensure a just distribution, and to prevent ruinous wars' with a balancing 'decentralization of power and the development of small, integrated communities where personal interaction can develop'.[21]

Above all, Stivers calls for a new world view. For Christians, this must emphasize a searching criticism of inherited exploitative views of nature, which have been based upon faulty interpretations of the Genesis stories of creation. It must also include rejection of the idolatries of growth, which Christians as well as humanists have tended to accept uncritically. For Christians, there is however a positive appeal: 'Concretely it is a call to basics: to faith; to human appeals for food, clothing, shelter, and health; to liberating structures that provide opportunities for human cooperation and creativity; to the throwing off of enslaving forces of affluence.' The resources of Christian faith include grounds for ultimate hope. 'The cross of the present crisis is not the final word. Out of death comes new life. Jesus Christ has overthrown the enslaving powers. We are free to change our ways without fear of judgment, for God is with us.'[22]

Stivers' overall conception is set more clearly in a Christian theological framework, and his judgments are generally more differentiated than those of Schumacher and Daly. Consequently, his ideological position seems more tentative and open. Nevertheless, he is in agreement on the fundamental point that the 'present narrow thrust for growth' must be slowed down, for it is based upon factual illusions and religious idolatries.

The Contributions of Economic Conservationism

Economic conservationism is relatively new as an option in economic ideology, and it is arguable that this viewpoint is not yet well enough developed to warrant our characterizing it is an ideology in quite the same sense as the other four. Whatever we may think about that matter of definition, it remains true that this new movement has made significant contributions to Christian ideological thinking. I wish to cite three points in particular.

First, economic conservationism has thrown a cup of cold water in the face of some persistent economic illusions of the past few generations. In some respects, we have been living in a fools' paradise. We have treated the finite world as if it were infinite. Our economic cost accounting has been based upon market forces, not upon realistic estimates of the long-range future. We have been the prodigal son, living riotously in the far country. The economic conservationists are here to remind us that if this continues for long we shall soon be eating husks with the hogs. Not that this movement is alone in sounding the alarm. The Club of Rome studies, the population experts, the agronomists, even the oil companies (in their own self-interested way) have sounded the alarm that we shall soon be up against the limits in a limited world. The economic conservationists have, however, gone beyond the technical experts in trying to help us organize this important fact into a value and policy frame of reference. We need to understand what the limits of earth *mean* to us and how we have organized our *thinking* about important economic questions wrongly. On the theory that it is better to face the painful truth and do something about it rather than squander the future recklessly, we we should be grateful to the economic conservationists.

Secondly, the movement has contributed a clear sense of the organic wholeness of life and our basic unity with nature. Like the ecology movement in general, it has insisted that nature is not simply there to be exploited. We belong to nature, and even in our mastery of the forces and materials of the natural world we remain subordinated to its processes. Economic conservationism therefore helps to overcome a certain alienation which crept into the relationship between humanity and the rest of nature with the industrial revolution. If there is a sense in which we exercise dominion over nature, it is as stewards; for we are responsible in those actions to the God who created nature and to the human family that will follow after us. In this sense, the economic conservation movement has, almost regardless of particular theological judgments, implied a deep respect for the fundamental goodness of God's whole creation. It can better enable us to look at the starry skies and the clear brooks and the trees and meadows and mountains with a clear conscience, recognizing that these wonders of nature also have their being from God.

Thirdly, economic conservationism insists upon the subordination of economic life to profounder human ends. This, too, is a point which may not be unique to this movement. But the Bouldings, Schumachers, Dalys, and Stivers have emphasized it persuasively. Ironically, this may be one reason why economic conservationism is not easily classified among or in relation to the other ideological viewpoints. In their writings, economic problems merge into the wider perspective of human culture and science – whereas in some other ideological perspectives there is a tendency to treat economic life as a self-contained unit or even as the single key to everything else.

Whether or not economic conservationism has provided us with a sufficiently clear and sufficiently comprehensive ideological perspective to guide us in dealing with economic problems, these contributions are of very great value.

Hard Questions

The very incompleteness of economic conservationism forces us to raise some hard questions, however. I wish to press four of them.

First, in a steady-state economy (proposed with variations by all of the writers we have considered), is it really possible to redistribute the world's goods equitably in any kind of foreseeable future? Bearing in mind the present vast disparities of wealth and income between the richest and poorest of lands, what happens when we freeze the sum total of wealth and income? Can we pry enough loose from the rich to bring the poor up to their level – or even anywhere near their level? A certain realism about the historic relationships of rich and poor intervenes to dictate the most plausible answer! Would a steady-state economy be, as some have suggested, like rich people kicking the ladder down behind them? Economic conservationists have wrestled with the question, but they have not yet issued compelling answers.

Secondly, would economic conservationism tend to inhibit the development of new energy sources which are not as wasteful as the old ones? The answer is, probably not, because this movement has placed great stress upon solar energy and other forms of natural energy (most of which ultimately derive from the sun) as our most promising way to fuel future economic activity without further depleting non-renewable energy sources. But the question goes deeper than this obvious answer. It is whether the mind-set of economic conservationism may tend to inhibit the full thrust of technological creativity needed to score the big breakthroughs. The history of technology suggests a pattern of movement toward as well as away from greater simplicity of design. Most of us are well aware of the latter. But technologists are equally conscious of how further and further refinement of major new ideas leads to greater simplicity of design efficiency and even of energy conservation. Note, for instance, the relative efficiency of transistor radios and later computer designs. A good deal of creative drive is necessary for such developments. Would this be undercut by the overall attitude of economic conservationism?

Thirdly, there is the somewhat similar question whether the discouragement of economic growth might also inhibit other forms of cultural creativity – thus leading toward social stagnation. This would not be offensive to some religious traditions, where the rhythms of existence are depicted in passive terms and where people are content to exist in whatever state they find themselves while awaiting death or final mystical absorption into Universal Being. But the Hebrew-Christian perspective has at its roots a more positive, constructive attitude toward the formation and celebration of culture. While some might wish to condemn the boundlessly creative energies released by this religious tradition historically, those who identify with it will continue to insist that creativity is an important human value. I do not believe there is anything in the economic conservationist position that should inevitably lead toward cultural stagnation. But the dominant rhetorical bent is away from activism, toward the acceptance of boundaries and limitations of future development. The movement does not seem to have developed values and goals clearly stimulating a permanently creative human spirit. (Schumacher's conception of the humanizing character of work might stand as an exception to this generalization.)

Fourthly, has economic conservationism yet addressed the hard political questions? The diagnosis proposed by these thinkers, by the Club of Rome studies, and by others suggests global interdependency. The major problems of resource scarcity, energy depletion, population over-expansion, hunger and so on are interlocked in a vast and vicious circle. Just as each of the dimensions of the overall problem tends to exacerbate each of the others, so our solutions must seek ways of affecting the whole. Moreover, the global systems cross national boundaries. Pure nationalism tends to exacerbate the problems, and purely nationalistic solutions are likely to fall short of the mark. But we have had far too little grappling with the political realities of this torn and conflicting world. Have the economic conservationists a profound political diagnosis of sufficient realism? How can the world be organized politically so as to provide for the stationary-state without embracing the risks of authoritarianism and imperialism? How can we get from a situation of international anarchy, which is profoundly complicated by the East-West conflict and Third World revolutionary movements, to a more humanizing political and economic structure transcending national boundaries?

Robert L. Heilbroner's *An Inquiry into the Human Prospect*[23] issues the challenge to and for economic conservationism in deeply pessimistic and, perhaps, realistic terms. In the light of the interlocking problems which we face, Heilbroner concludes that the future will hold 'sustained and convulsive change as the inescapable lot of human society for a very long period to come'.[24] The political prescription for this unhappy prospect, which Heilbroner himself to some extent advocates, is a very substantial increase of authoritarianism. Democracy of sorts may continue to be possible, but only on the condition of a high degree of social self-discipline – which is in itself not a likely prospect. 'As I examine the prospect ahead,' he writes, 'I not only predict but I prescribe a centralization of power as the only means by which our threatened and dangerous civilization will make way for its successor. Yet we live at a time when I am profoundly suspicious of the further gathering of political power. So, too, my analysis leads me to place my hopes for the long-term survival of man on his susceptibility to appeals to national identity and to his willingness to accept authority.'[25] The provisional model he advances is that of the monastery or, on a large-scale, perhaps that of the People's Republic of China.

By and large, economic conservationists have evidenced no willingness to advance a political analysis paralleling in depth and urgency their analysis of the crisis of industrial civilization as it relates to resources and environment. Without this political dimension, their ideological frame of reference will remain incomplete.

9

Ideology and Beyond

> I see us free, therefore, to return to some of the most sure and certain principles of religion and traditional virtue – that avarice is a vice, that the exaction of usury is a misdemeanour, and the love of money is detestable, that those walk most truly in the paths of virtue and sane wisdom who take least thought for the morrow. We shall once more value ends above means and prefer the good to the useful. We shall honour those who can teach us how to pluck the hour and the day virtuously and well, the delightful people who are capable of taking direct enjoyment in things, the lilies of the field who toil not, neither do they spin.
>
> John Maynard Keynes

What does the debate over economic ideology all add up to? We do well, as we conclude this exploration, to recall two things: the purpose of economics and the function of ideology in ethical thinking.

Lord Keynes' statement from 'Economic Possibilities for our Grandchildren', which heads this chapter, is a good reminder of the first. He may not have been right in supposing that our economic problems would all one day be solved so we could turn to better things. But he was clearly right in the underlying assumption that 'man does not live by bread alone'. The ultimate purpose of economic life is to liberate us from being dominated by scarcity and to provide us with the conditions necessary to a fully human existence. It is to make possible the higher ends of human brotherhood and creativity in response to the boundless goodness of God.

And the function of ideology? It is to give overall organization to our thinking on social, economic, political matters so that our values and our perceptions of practical possibility can be united in a single guiding perspective. But the true possibilities of ideological thinking can be distorted if we become blinded to plain facts and unexpected truths. As we indicated in the first chapter, ideologies can be most useful if they are held presumptively. An ideology serves in this way to help us locate the burden of proof. We will make our moral decisions in harmony with our guiding ideological perspective unless, upon careful examination, there seems to be sufficient reason for abandoning it.

Now that we have explored the five main economic ideologies of the present world-wide debate, is there a clear choice to be made?

We have seen certain contributions in each, along with potential blindspots. Overall, the ideologies of Marxist Communism and laissez faire capitalism seem to have fatal flaws which would prevent a Christian from espousing either without serious reservations. The other three – social market capitalism, democratic socialism, and economic conservationism – are generally capable of preserving the contributions of the first two without being burdened by their major flaws. Each of the three can be deeply committed to human rights and political democracy. Each can envisage the use of economic production for the welfare of human beings in the good society. Each is potentially receptive to most of the values which claim the allegiance of Christians, and each can encompass safeguards against sinfulness. Their major differences centre upon the degree to which we must hitch the wagon of economics to incentives based upon selfishness in order to get the work done and upon the extent to which we must base economic policy upon the limits of earth.

Some will say that we might as well declare democratic socialism the preferable starting point, letting the burden of proof be borne by social market capitalism or economic conservationism. If democratic socialism were our governing presumption, then we should at least be clear in saying that the presumption will be against appealing to selfish motives and we shall not adopt policies requiring such an appeal except when it is clearly necessary for the sake of overall well-being. Moreover, we should presume in favour of equality in the distribution of economic benefits unless it can be shown that specific inequalities are truly necessary. Our democratic socialism will have to be refined. We shall have to develop creative answers to the potential problems of overconcentration of power, but we shall be particularly wary of permitting major concentrations of power to accumulate in private hands for potentially exploitative purposes. At that point, we shall require every form of capitalism to bear a particularly difficult burden of proof.

Of course, the debate between democratic socialism and what we have called economic conservationism would not be so clear-cut. The whole agenda of economic conservationism could, in fact, simply be incorporated into a socialist perspective. (Barry Commoner has in effect done so in his exploration of the energy problem.[1]) But a presumptive distinction does in fact remain. It can be stated in this way. When the traditional democratic socialist has to choose between equality and public control on the one hand and conservationist objectives on the other hand, he or she is likely to force the conservationist position to bear the burden of proof. Economic conservationists may have had some questions about the crash development of North Sea oil, but socialists in the British Labour government could hardly have avoided thinking of the oil discoveries as a godsend to be exploited as quickly as was feasible in order to provide resources to help build a strong and healthy socialist society. Similarly, typical social market capitalists tend to put the burden of proof against anything contrary to increasing productivity and production. Economic conservationists on the other hand, while they may share many of the objectives of the socialists or social market capitalists, will place a presumption against anything that seems a threat to the environment or a depletion of non-renewable resources.

Social market capitalists, attracted by the present accomplishments and future possibilities of the mixed economy, will tend to say that the burden of proof must be borne by major, untried innovations – such as any attempt to leap immediately into socialism. This form of ideological presumption will not in principle resist innovation, but it will be reluctant to take more than one step at a time. Its focus will be on concrete improvements in the human situation rather than upon an overall structural change.

While one or another of these three ideologies may seem the

more conservative and one or another more radical and innovative, all are in conflict with the dominant ideological tendencies in the United States. For all three depend upon a much more direct involvement by government in economic life than dominant current ideology permits. None of the three ideologies is afraid, in principle, of a considerable extension of governmental participation in the economy – including governmental investments in the private sector and the outright socialization of major segments of the economy, such as health care. And none, in principle, resists a strong government role in protecting the environment and planning for effective future use of scarce resources. Social market capitalism, the least socialistic of the three, does not place the burden of proof against government involvement in the economy, but rather against complete exclusion of private ownership in the means of production.

I do not believe we yet know enough about the diverse possible economic futures to exclude any of the three ideological forms. My own inclination, over the long run, is more toward democratic socialism than toward the other two. I would at least agree with John Bennett that we live at a time when the socialist question needs to be pressed.[2] I take it this means that, up to a point, other alternatives are forced to bear a burden of proof. For example, why should not the oil companies be nationalized or, at least, placed under very tight supervision in an overall energy policy? And why should there not be a comprehensive public health and medical care programme in countries like the United States as there is in countries like Great Britain? The frontier between democratic socialism and economic conservationism is less easily defined, but it seems to me that when an apparently clear choice between social justice and resource conservation is factually before us, the burden of proof should be borne by the latter, not the former. I have two reasons for this. First, because conservationist rhetoric is more likely to be used as an ideological mask (in the pejorative sense) for continuing injustice than the other way around. Second, because I believe it more likely that a social democratic state would be able to manage the conservation question over the long run – whereas the economic conservationist position does not yet have a clearly articulated political philosophy by which to deal with the social justice questions.

But clearly all three of these ideological frameworks are such that many Christians will be found supporting each. There could be great value in a period of several years' dialogue among the three, and much will be gained by the flourishing of actual economic models illustrating each. The coming dialogue must touch upon many of the issues which have already been discussed in this book. But three overall questions may be particularly important: the question of economic and political power, the question of the possibilities and limits to human nature, and the question of the possibilities and limits of the natural world and universe. Each may be worth a few additional comments here.

The Dialogue on Power

Any modern economy must have a vast and, in some sense growing, capital base – the machinery and plants, the productive capacity which makes it possible to create the goods used by society. As we saw at the conclusion of Chapter 5, the wealth entailed in the capital base will be viewed differently by different ideologies. Presently it is defined as 'surplus value' by Marxists in order to emphasize that it was created by workers but stolen from them by capitalists as private property. Laissez faire capitalists on the other hand, will describe the same capital wealth as the accumulated savings of those who have worked particularly hard or creatively and at the same time refrained from consuming all they have earned. Whether the wealth of the capital base is primarily 'owned' by individuals and corporations privately or by society as a whole through the state, it is still essentially the same thing: the productive capacity used by workers to create necessary and desirable goods. For this reason, some social market capitalists, including Lord Keynes, have concluded that it really does not matter much who 'owns' the productive wealth as long as it is managed in directions determined by the market and democratic decision.

The democratic socialist, on the other hand, argues that it does matter for four reasons. First, because the owner will have a vastly greater potential for personal consumption. Secondly, because with private ownership production can only occur when there is potential profitability. Thirdly, because concentrations of private wealth are irresponsible forms of power which make it possible for a small number of people to dominate economic decision making, almost regardless of governmental regulation. And fourthly, because economic power drifts so easily over into political power. Private economic power on a large and concentrated scale makes it much more difficult for the whole society to control its own economic destiny.

Those who are persuaded by the arguments of social market capitalism may reject this reasoning on two grounds. First, on the supposition that privately-owned concentrations of productive wealth are more conducive to the enterprising spirit (the supposition being that more production occurs when at least a major part of the economy is free to function as it will). Second, that competing private centres of power may in fact be a healthy counterweight to an otherwise overpowering government.

Social market capitalism seeks to have the best of both worlds, the private and the public. Democratic socialism considers it an illusion to suppose that public power can coexist with private corporate power without the latter dominating the former.

Dialogue on these points can be creative, partly because in principle both sides are wholly committed to the democratic accountability of social power. The question becomes, then, a largely empirical one. In the final analysis, much should therefore depend upon how the multinational corporations and the rest of the private sector actually does behave in coming years. If the multinationals do develop further along the lines of irresponsible power which have been laid out so clearly by, for example, ITT, and if it generally proves impossible to manage the modern economy without substantial unemployment and/or inflation – then the honest advocate of social market capitalism will give more and more to democratic socialism. At the same time, we may hope to begin to see some experiments with democratic socialism. And if the latter in fact seems unable to develop without stuffiness and stagnation, then the democratic socialists should become more accepting of some kind of creative private sector. Hopefully a number of the Marxist countries will begin to evolve more in the democratic socialist direction.

The Dialogue on Human Nature

It is interesting how much of the present ideological debate comes back to the question of the possibilities and limitations of human nature. The debate between democratic socialism and social market capitalism does not bring this into sharp focus, since both accept the positive, creative side of human nature and both acknowledge tendencies toward self-centredness which need to be hedged and checked. Still, there may be an important difference in degree over the question of incentives. Is it ultimately possible to fuel an economy on creative devotion to the common good or is it necessary to appeal to the self-interest of people to get them to exert themselves? Perhaps we might all agree that it would be a good thing to have a society in which people really did work together generously and co-operatively. The question is whether such a society is possible.

Many supporters of socialism have made a good deal out of the recent experiences of China and Cuba, two countries which have given much attention to the encouragement of a new human type to emerge on a foundation of Marxist socialism. Evidence from both these situations remains contradictory and, in any case, it is not clear how exportable their particular social models will prove to be. Most of us can certainly cite smaller groups much closer to home in which people have seemed thoroughly 'socialized' in the sense of their full devotion to the common good. Again, it is a question whether this can be generalized at the level of society as a whole and over a long time span. On the other hand, there is plenty of evidence of human societies, capitalist and socialist alike, in which mean, self-seeking individualism is a major force.

Christians, participating in this debate, will want to be realistic about the darker side of human nature. At the same time, it would be a curious thing indeed if they found themselves placing their major emphasis upon the motive power of selfishness while at the same time trying to overcome that same force by witnessing to the power of God's redeeming grace! Would it not seem strange for Christians to be less affirmative about human possibilities than Maoists? To be sure, Christians may have deeper insight into the sources of human sinfulness than Maoists do; they may recognize that evil is not finally to be cured through any amount of social manipulation. Nevertheless, they presumably have some countervailing faith in the power of God, active in history through human beings for his good purposes. Surely they must not concede too much to the power of evil by structuring social processes so that people do what they do for the wrong reasons.

Here I want to interject that capitalism, despite what its most ardent defenders themselves say, may not be based altogether upon selfishness. One can be engaged in business life for very high motives. But every form of capitalism, including social market capitalism, is susceptible to a peculiar degree to the encouragement of baser human motives. Those who continue to support social market capitalism need to be especially watchful at this point. Of course, socialists must also be wary lest they give too much opportunity to the self-seeking of a 'new class' in a socialist situation. In both cases, it may arise that particular policies must be adopted which rest upon selfish incentives – but such policies should be forced to bear a burden of proof.

Clearly, in our time, there is need for greater emphasis upon the human capacity to build the co-operative commonwealth – whether its economy is socialist or some kind of mixed economy. There is a limit to how much more selfishness modern Western society can stand without tearing itself apart.

The Dialogue on the Limits of Earth

It has been evident at several points on the preceding chapter and in this one that there is a certain awkwardness in relating economic conservationism to the other economic ideologies on the same conceptual levels. Nevertheless, economic conservationism has pressed in a new way the dialogue on ecology. The other ideologies tend to presuppose an earth without built-in limits, and we are now reminded that it in fact has limits we ignore only at our peril. It would, I think, be possible for a consistent democratic socialism or a consistent social market capitalism to accept the main conclusions of the conservationists right into their ideological frame of reference. For the social market capitalist, the conservationist agenda would become one of the important areas for governmental intervention and regulation. Typical social market capitalism would have to modify its economic growth orientation substantially, but even there growth can be re-defined in relation to conservationist objectives. For the democratic socialist, the conservationist agenda would be incorporated even more easily into the policy objectives guiding governmental economic planning.

There are, however, two questions which remain moot enough to stimulate serious dialogue in the years to come. First is the factual question, just what is our situation. How *much* oil, really, is there yet undiscovered? How serious *is* the threat of aerosol sprays and supersonic transport planes to the atmospheric ozone layer? *Can* we in fact develop a safe power source in nuclear fission? To what event *is* solar energy a potential solution to our energy problems? How much food *can* be grown around the world without depleting soils? What *is* the population carrying-capacity of the earth at a quality-of-life level consistent with genuine human fulfilment? And so on. Only a fool would pretend to have definitive answers to all such questions. And only a fool would treat such questions as unimportant.

The other question has to do with the extent of our obligation to future generations and to the non-human aspects of nature. To a considerable extent, this is a question for ethicists and theologians to wrestle with. The built-in limits of earth mean that not every potential human being will in fact be born to experience the joys and wonders and sorrows of life. We are learning, unfortunately, that neither fate nor providence alone will decide how the trade-offs between the happiness and well-being of the present generation and the future prospects for life and happiness of generations yet unborn will be handled. Clearly, it is not the unhappy lot and obligation of the present generation to subordinate everything for the future. At the same time, Christians and all thoughtful people whether or not they are Christians, must think of the human moral community in historical as well as geographical terms. We belong to a family of humankind existing throughout the world and through past and future time. To the impertinent question, What has posterity ever done for me?, we must reply, it has done nothing *yet*, but an important part of the meaning of our human existence is that it *will* do something of inestimable value for us: it will register and perpetuate the value and influence of our lives in the ongoing stream of human history.

We also owe a moral debt to the non-human aspects of nature, a debt which transcends our purely utilitarian dependence. There is a kind of worship-of-nature cultism which need not detain us. Nor need we pause too long over the question whether or not humanity is the highest form of nature. I would answer that it is, and without much hesitation, because humankind is that aspect of nature we know to be capable of transcending nature in thought and feeling. As the Hebrews said, we are made in the image of God; we are not simply reflective mechanisms of the natural order. Nor do we need to feel too apologetic in the exploitation of nature if, by that term we mean the *uses* of nature for human ends. But having registered these points, do we not also need to come to terms with the fact that is both descriptive and moral that nature is also vaster than man? To put this in religious terms, I should like to say that nature is both the basis of human existence and at the same time an important part of the self-disclosure of God. I do not believe in worshipping the sunset and the mountains and trees and stars, but I do believe that the beauties and rhythms of nature can be celebrated in worship and faith as part of the self-disclosure of the loving God. The economic conservationists, when they press us beyond the narrow utilitarianisms of economic life, help to remind us of such things.

The Importance of Non-Economic Factors in Economics

We need not be troubled by having to conclude without final answers. Economics is not an exact science. Only in the minds of some badly insulated economists does economic life still seem to be an altogether independent equilibrium of economic forces. Man is not *homo economicus*, finally, although economic life is very important to his well-being.

We have surely observed throughout this exploration that historical and cultural factors are very important in shaping our economic attitudes and expectations. When all is said and done, it may be that peculiar historical circumstances and culturally inherited values and beliefs have more to do with the shape of economic life than do any universal economic motives. George Dalton, who writes both as an economist and as an anthropologist, argues that traditional attributes of culture and social organization – that which differentiates Hungarians from Russians, Yugoslavians from Albanians, Japanese from Spaniards, Germans from English – will count more than capitalist or socialist institutions in determining success or failure of Third World nations to industrialize and develop; that communist China will do better than communist Cuba for the same reasons that capitalist Japan has done better than capitalist Philippines; that semi-socialist Israel will continue to do better than socialist Egypt and Syria – not because of American public and private aid, which, in any case, hardly offsets Arab oil – but because the Israelis are Europeans whose technical skills and public administration are more effective than those of the Arab Middle East; and that socialist Guinea and Tanzania will not do any better than capitalist Ivory Coast and Nigeria.[3]

Dalton's specific judgments would require further analysis. But this overall observation needs to be taken seriously by all people who are concerned about economic matters. To say this is not to play down the importance of economics; rather, it is to heighten it. For economic matters are interwoven into the whole fabric of human existence. Economists can help us greatly, as we have seen, in understanding the logical and quantifiable relationships among economic facts. They can help us analyse past, present, and future economic problems on the basis of technical factors. But economic analysis and prediction also rest upon human values and human decision making of a non-technical sort. In confronting these wider human considerations, the economist becomes a lay person like all the rest of us.

This observation brings our discussion full circle to the points with which we began in the first chapter. Economics cannot be divorced from morality, and it is time to repair the damage which that pretension has caused in our social thinking. Professor Joan Robinson, herself an internationally renowned economist, makes this point on behalf of her fellow economists:

> The economics of the laissez-faire school purported to abolish the moral problem by showing that the pursuit of self-interest by each individual rebounds to the benefit of all. The task of the generation now in rebellion is to reassert the authority of morality over technology; the business of social scientists is to help them to see both how necessary and how difficult that task is going to be.[4]

Agreeing with her, Christians and all other persons of good will must seek to influence economic life everywhere on the basis of their noblest visions of the purposes and possibilities of existence – treating economic science as a servant, not the master of the enterprise.

Notes

1. Is Economics beyond Morality?

1. Book V. Chapter II.

2. See H. Richard Niebuhr, *Radical Monotheism and Western Culture*, Harper & Row, New York, 1960.

3. Named after economist A. W. Phillips, the 'Phillips Curve' attempts to quantify this relationship. In general, it assumes that the higher the rate of inflation goes the less employment, and vice versa. The variables affecting this are complex, but the Curve seems to say that the only way to dampen inflation is by creating unemployment, and the only way to have full employment is by risking or tolerating substantial inflation. Not all economists accept this representation.

4. See US Senate Finance Committee, *The Multinational Corporation and the World Economy* (Washington, DC: US Government Printing Office, 1973). Richard J. Barnet and Ronald E. Muller note that 'If we compare the annual sales of corporations with the gross national product of countries for 1973, we discover that General Motors is bigger than Switzerland, Pakistan, and South Africa; that Royal Dutch Shell is bigger than Iran, Venezuela, and Turkey; and that Goodyear Tyre is bigger than Saudi Arabia. The average growth rate of the most successful global corporations is two to three times that of most advanced countries, including the United States. It is estimated that global corporations already have more than $200 billion in physical assets under their control. . . . In the process of developing a new world, the managers of firms like General Motors, IBM, Pepsico, General Electric, Pfizer, Shell, Volkswagen, Exxon, and a few hundred others are making daily business decisions which have more impact than those of most sovereign governments on where people live; what work, if any, they will do; what they will eat, drink, and wear; what sorts of knowledge schools and universities will encourage; and what kind of society their children will inherit.' *Global Reach: The Power of the Multinational Corporations*, Simon & Schuster, New York, 1974, p. 15.

5. Nasrollah S. Fatemi and Gail W. Williams, *Multinational Corporations*, A. S. Barnes, Cranbury, New Jersey, 1975, p. 58.

6. Barnet and Muller, *Global Reach*, p. 364.

7. Quoted by Harry M. Johnson, 'Ideology and the Social System', *Encyclopedia of the Social Sciences*, Macmillan, New York, 1968, p. 76.

2. *Can We Avoid Ideological Thinking?*

1. Howard E. Kershner, 'The Inevitable Bankruptcy of the Socialist State', in F. A. von Hayek et al. (eds.), *Toward Liberty: Essays in Honor of Ludwig von Mises*, Vol. II, Menlo Park, California, Institute for Humane Studies 1971.

2. Ludwig von Mises, *The Free and Prosperous Commonwealth: An Exposition of the Ideas of Classical Liberalism*, tr., Ralph Raico, D. Van Nostrand Co., Princeton, New Jersey 1962, 1927, pp. 88–89.

3. Ibid., p. 90.

4. Ibid., pp. 72–73.

5. Oskar Lange, 'On the Economic Theory of Socialism', in Harry Townsend (ed.), *Price Theory: Selected Readings*, Penguin Books 1971, 1936–37, pp. 32 ff.

6. Friedrich Engels, *Socialism: Utopian and Scientific* (1880), ET, Edward Aveling (1892). This small book was originally published as three of the chapters of Engels' *Anti-Duhring*. The degree to which Engels fully reflects the subtlety of Marx's own thought is a matter of controversy among Marxist scholars. The important thing, however, is that the Marxist movement itself has generally regarded this writing to be among the definitive points of departure for understanding socialism as a science.

7. V. I. Lenin, *Imperialism, The Highest Stage of Capitalism*, Foreign Languages Publishing House, Moscow, n.d.; first published 1917.

8. Maurice Dobb, *Political Economy and Capitalism: Some Essays in Economic Tradition*, Routledge, rev. ed. 1940, pp. 256–257.

9. Maurice Dobb, *Capitalism Yesterday and Today*, Lawrence & Wishart, London 1958, pp. 51–52.

10. Ibid.

11. Dobb, *Political Economy and Capitalism*, p. 245.

12. See especially Paul A. Baron and Paul M. Sweezy, *Monopoly Capital: An Essay on the American Economic and Social Order*, Monthly Review Press, New York 1966 and Paul M. Sweezy, *Modern Capitalism and Other Essays*, Monthly Review Press, New York 1972.

13. On these points see Michael Harrington, *Socialism*, Saturday

Review Press, New York 1972, Chapter XIII, part I, in which this socialist acknowledges the economic strength of the advanced capitalist economies.

14. Joan Robinson, 'The Model of an Expanding Economy', *The Economic Journal*, March 1952, pp. 42–43.

15. Daniel Bell, *The End of Ideology: On the Exhaustion of Political Ideas in the Fifties*, The Free Press, Glencoe, Illinois, 1960, p. 16.

16. Ibid., p. 375.

17. From the Preface to the English Edition of Karl Mannheim, *Ideology and Utopia*, Harcourt, Brace, & World, New York 1962, 1936.

18. In his classical analysis of ideology, Karl Mannheim reminds us that ideological taint is not necessarily a conscious phenomenon: 'mental structures are inevitably differently formed in different social settings' (p. 265). My own use of the term 'ideology' is broader than Mannheim's in that I include in the term what he calls 'utopia'. I also differ from Mannheim in seeking conscious acceptance of and control over ideology in our ethical reasoning. See *A Christian Method of Moral Judgment*, SCM Press, and Westminster Press 1976, pp. 182 ff.

19. Joseph A. Schumpeter, *History of Economic Analysis*, Oxford University Press, New York 1954, p. 36.

20. H. Richard Niebuhr's brilliant little book, *Radical Monotheism and Western Culture* illuminates the meaning of the transcendence of God in terms which could be taken seriously by non-Christians as well as by those who are already committed in some way to Christian faith.

3. *Moral Foundations*

1. John Rawls, *A Theory of Justice*, Harvard University Press 1971. Also Oxford University Press, London 1972.

2. Ibid., pp. 14–15.

3. Ibid., p. 15.

4. Ibid., p. 529.

5. Quoted by Robert L. Heilbroner, *An Inquiry into the Human Prospect*, W. W. Norton, New York, 1975 edition, p. 170.

6. See L. Harold DeWolf, *Responsible Freedom: Guidelines to Christian Action*, Harper & Row, New York 1971, and Joseph Haroutunian, *God with Us: A Theology of Transpersonal Life*, Westminster Press, Philadelphia 1965.

7. Karl Barth, *Church Dogmatics* III/1, T. & T. Clark, Edinburgh 1958.

8. Philip Wogaman, *Guaranteed Annual Income: The Moral Issues,* Abingdon Press, New York and Nashville 1968, pp. 71–73.

4. *The Case for Marxism*

1. *Capital,* Vol. I, Chapter XXVI, tr., Samuel Moore and Edward Aveling.

2. The reader will recall that Marx was only 26 in that year and that the *Communist Manifesto* was written in 1847. Most of Marx's own writings came after 1850. The first volume of his greatest economic work, *Das Kapital,* was published in 1867, with the second and third volumes edited by Engels and published after Marx's own death. It is an interesting scholarly problem whether the early writings are fully consistent with the later, but they may reasonably be enough so for our purposes.

3. Third Manuscript, T.B.Bottomore translation, in Erich Fromm, *Marx's Concept of Man,* Frederick Ungar, New York 1961, p. 151.

4. *Daily Tribune,* 18 February 1853.

5. *Toward the Critique of Hegel's Philosophy of Right,* selections in Lewis S. Feuer (ed.), *Marx and Engels Basic Writings on Politics and Philosophy,* Doubleday Anchor, New York 1959, p. 263.

6. Denys L. Munby, *Christianity and Economic Problems,* Macmillan, London 1956, p. 30.

7. In Richard C. Edwards, et al. (eds.), *The Capitalist System: A Radical Analysis of American Society,* Prentice-Hall, Englewood Cliffs, New Jersey 1972, p. 134.

8. Herbert Marcuse, *An Essay on Liberation,* Penguin Books, Harmondsworth, England 1969, pp. 69–70.

9. Ibid.

10. Ibid., p. 85.

11. Baron and Sweezy, *Monopoly Capitalism,* p. 157.

12. Ibid.

13. Ibid., p. 158.

14. Ibid., p. 349.

15. Ibid., p. 353.

16. A Czech public opinion poll in October, 1969 disclosed that only 3% of the people identified themselves positively with the 1948–1968 regime and that the Soviet invasion of August 1968 was considered to be one of the most unfortunate periods in Czech history. Vladimir V. Kusin, *The Intellectual Origins of the Prague Spring: The Development of Reformist Ideas in Czechoslovakia 1956–1967,* Cambridge University Press 1971, p. 16.

17. Harrington, *Socialism,* p. 340.

18. Some eminent Marxist economists, including Professor Mau-

rice Dobb, continue to regard this element in Marxism as crucial. See his *Theories of Value and Distribution Since Adam Smith: Ideology and Economic Theory*, Cambridge University Press 1973.

19. Joan Robinson, *An Essay on Marxian Economics*, second edition, Macmillan, New York 1966, p. 22.

20. Ibid.

21. The labour theory of value, which Marx largely took over from Ricardo, is confusing because while it seems to be a theory of prices it cannot explain the rise or fall of prices in the actual market. Supposedly items will all ultimately be priced on the basis of the amount of labour that has gone into them (and into the machines needed to produce them). But consumers may decide not to buy some things at any price regardless of how much work they have entailed. And they may buy some other things which have almost no labour invested in them at all – such as the 'pet rocks' that were successfully marketed in the United States in 1975 at about $4 apiece. Moreover, the theory does not really account for differences in native ability – even when units of labour are treated as if all labour were unskilled. The labour theory doubtless does refer to an important element in the creation of economic value; but it can hardly pass muster as an adequate theory since by itself it does not explain actual economic events and relationships.

5. *The Case for Laissez Faire Capitalism*

1. Ludwig von Mises, *The Ultimate Foundation of Economic Science: An Essay on Method*, D. Van Nostrand Co., Princeton, New Jersey 1962, p. 122.

2. Feuer (ed.), *Marx and Engels Basic Writings*, p. 10.

3. J. A. Schumpeter, *Capitalism, Socialism and Democracy*, Harper & Row, New York, third edition, 1950, 1962, p. 64.

4. John C. Bennett, 'Capitalism, Ethics, and Morality', in National Industrial Conference Board, *The Future of Capitalism*, Macmillan, New York 1967.

5. Milton Friedman, *Capitalism and Freedom*, University of Chicago Press 1962, p. 12.

6. Ibid.

7. Ibid., p. 13.

8. Von Mises, *The Ultimate Foundation of Economic Science*, p. 108.

9. Max Weber, *The Protestant Ethic and the Spirit of Capitalism*, tr., Talcott Parsons, Charles Scribner's Sons, New York 1958, 1904–5.

10. This is loose terminology because the word 'profit' refers to a specific economic relationship and the word 'motive' suggests a

universal aspect of human psychology. More accurately, we should speak of the 'profit incentive', since the system uses profit as a specific incentive. There is an excellent discussion of the profit incentive in Walter G. Muelder, *Religion and Economic Responsibility*, Scribner's Sons, New York 1953, pp. 78ff.

11. Cf. Ayn Rand, *The Virtue of Selfishness: A New Concept of Egoism*, New American Library, New York 1964.

12. *The Ultimate Foundation of Economic Science*, p. 128.

13. Ibid., pp. 75–76.

14. Joan Robinson, *Freedom and Necessity: An Introduction to the Study of Society*, Allen & Unwin 1970, p. 116.

15. Bennett, 'Capitalism, Ethics, and Morality', in *The Future of Capitalism*, p. 162.

16. *Monopoly Capitalism*, p. 278.

17. Foreword in *The Future of Capitalism*, p. xvi. The income figures referred to should, of course, be corrected in terms of the 1967 date of publication.

18. *The Ultimate Foundation of Economic Science*, p. 59.

19. *The Free and Prosperous Commonwealth*, p. 29.

20. *Capitalism, Socialism and Democracy*, p. 67.

21. In this connection, it is worth noting that in his famous book *The Other America: Poverty in the United States*, Macmillan, New York 1962, Michael Harrington mentioned the general similarity of clothing in the United States as one of the reasons why poor people are so frequently 'invisible' to those who are more prosperous.

22. Friedman, *Capitalism and Freedom*, pp. 9–10.

23. *The Ultimate Foundation of Economic Science*, pp. 122–123.

24. Ibid., p. 113.

25. This was analysed with great care a quarter of a century ago by K. William Kapp, *The Social Costs of Private Enterprise*, Harvard University Press 1950.

26. A. B. Atkinson, *The Economics of Inequality*, The Clarendon Press, Oxford 1975, pp. 136ff.

27. Ibid., pp. 138–39.

28. Quoted by Lord Stamp, *Christianity and Economics*, Macmillan, London 1939, p. 65, from *Economic Consequences of the Peace*, p. 17.

6. *The Case for Social Market Capitalism*

1. Paul Samuelson, *Economics*, ninth edition, McGraw-Hill, New York 1973, p. 845.

2. The Programme adopted by the SDP at Bad Godesberg conference specifically affirmed economic competition and a market

system with the formula: 'as much competition as possible – as much planning as necessary'. It held it to be a central task of all economic policy to bring great concentrations of economic power under control, and it acknowledged that concentrations of economic power in the hands of the state are also dangerous. See F. R. Allemann, 'Farewell to Marx', in *Encounter*, vol. 14, no. 3, March 1960, pp. 67–9

3. Quoted by Harrington, *Socialism*, p. 268.

4. See his *Christianity and Economic Problems* and his Foreword in Denys Munby (ed.), *Economic Growth in World Perspective*, SCM Press 1966.

5. *Christianity and Economic Problems*, p. 245.

6. Ibid.

7. Ibid., p. 203.

8. Ibid., p. 163.

9. Ibid., p. 235.

10. George Dalton, *Economic Systems and Society: Capitalism, Communism and the Third World*, Penguin Books Ltd, Harmondsworth, England 1974, p. 144.

11. Samuelson, *Economics*, p. 203.

12. Ibid.

13. Compared with the other Western democracies, America lags behind most visibly in terms of health care delivery, and aid to such cultural activities as music, art, and theatre. On the other hand, America's accomplishments in publicly supported education at all levels has been most impressive.

14. J. K. Galbraith, *Money: Whence it Came. Where it Went*, André Deutsch 1975, especially pp. 268–312.

15. Galbraith, *The New Industrial State*, Houghton-Mifflin, Boston, 1967.

16. John Hicks, *The Crisis in Keynesian Economics*, Basil Blackwell, Oxford 1974.

17. Ibid., p. 25.

18. Ibid., pp. 64–65.

19. Richard Kahn, *On Re-Reading Keynes*, Oxford University Press 1974, p. 19.

20. Ibid.

21. R. J. Barnet and R. E. Muller, *Global Reach*, p. 17.

22. Stuart Holland, *The Socialist Challenge*, Quartet Books, London 1975, p. 140.

23. *Global Reach*, p. 42.

7. The Case for Democratic Socialism

1. This brief characterization of the Czech reform movement and its aftermath is partly based upon three personal visits to that country in recent years.

2. One of the historians of the reform movement remarked that 'There is every reason to believe that the Czechoslovak reform movement believed it could realize its programme within the context of Communism and alliance with the Soviets. It was Moscow, not Prague, which said – perhaps proved – the contrary.' Galia Golan, *Czechoslovak Reform Movement*, Cambridge University Press 1972. p. 329.

3. See especially US Senate Select Committee to Study Governmental Operations with Respect to Intelligence Activities, *Hearings, Thursday, Dec. 4 and Friday, Dec. 5, 1975*, 'Covert Action in Chile', US Government Printing Office, Washington DC, pp. 144ff. for documentation of the US role in the period leading up to the coup against the Allende government. We should avoid drawing direct parallels between the Czechoslovakian and Chilean situations, since the Soviet invasion was overt and military while American efforts to undermine the Allende government in Chile were indirect and primarily economic. Nevertheless, left alone each of these situations might well have provided us with useful new models of democratic socialism.

4. Albert Fried and Ronald Sanders (eds.), *Socialist Thought: A Documentary History*, University of Edinburgh Press 1964, p. 51.

5. Michael Harrington, *The Accidental Century*, Macmillan, New York 1965.

6. William Coats, *God in Public*, Eerdmans, Grand Rapids, Michigan 1974, p. 178.

7. Nyerere, *'Ujamaa': The Basis of African Socialism*, Tanganyika Standard Ltd, Dar es Salaam 1962, p. 8.

8. Ibid.

9. Ibid., p. 1.

10. See especially Harrington, *Socialism, The Accidental Century*, and *Toward A Democratic Left*, Pelican, Baltimore 1968. The first of these is his most definitive volume.

11. *Socialism*, p. 185.

12. Ibid., p. 177.

13. Ibid., p. 371.

14. Ibid., p. 306. Actually, this suggestion is less radical than that of Andrew Carnegie who, for the sake of equal opportunity in economic competition, advocated the outright abolition of inheritance.

15. *The Socialist Challenge* is Holland's principal writing.

16. See, for example, John Eagleson (ed.), *Christians and Socialism: Documentation of the Christians for Socialism Movement in Latin America*, Orbis Books, Maryknoll, New York 1975.

17. It is also worthy of note that Karl Barth, like Paul Tillich, was strongly attracted to socialism as a young man and that he never abandoned this position even though it did not bulk large in his later writings. Some Barthian scholars contend that the socialist commitment profoundly shaped his whole theological enterprise. Others disagree. He certainly did not think of his commitment as an ideological one, although it seems to me that he was involved in ideology in the senses in which I am defining that term. For an interesting introduction and conflicting interpretations of Barth's socialist views, see George Hunsinger, ed. and trans., *Karl Barth and Radical Politics*, Westminster Press, Philadelphia 1976.

18. Von Mises, *The Ultimate Foundation of Economic Science*, p. 132.

19. *The Socialist Challenge*, p. 285.

20. Besides demonstrating a great openness to socialist ideas, John C. Bennett warns against 'the total union of economic and political power, which 'could well be more oppressive than some degree of pluralism among private economic empires that coexist with a democratic state'. He urges us 'to press the socialistic questions even though' we 'do not accept ready-made socialistic answers'. *The Radical Imperative: From Theology to Social Ethics*, Westminster Press, Philadelphia 1975, p. 156.

8. *The Case for Economic Conservationism*

1. E. F. Schumacher, *Small is Beautiful*, Blond and Briggs Ltd, London 1973. Quotations are from the Abacus edition, London 1974.
2. Ibid., p. 23.
3. Ibid., p. 11.
4. Ibid., p. 25.
5. Ibid., p. 45.
6. Ibid., p. 48.
7. Ibid., pp. 150f.
8. Ibid., p. 179.
9. Ibid., p. 212.
10. Ibid., pp. 216–17.
11. Ibid., p. 217.
12. Herman E. Daly (ed.), *Toward A Steady-State Economy*, W. H. Freeman, San Francisco 1974. The Introduction and two of the essays in this volume are by Professor Daly. See also the article, 'The

Entropy Law and the Economic Problem', by Nicholas Georgescu-Roegen, ibid., pp. 37ff.

13. Ibid., p. 46.
14. Daly, *Toward A Steady-State Economy*, p. 152.
15. Ibid., p. 23.
16. Ibid.
17. Ibid., p. 21.
18. Robert L. Stivers, *The Sustainable Society: Ethics and Economic Growth*, Westminster Press, Philadelphia 1976.
19. Ibid., p. 187.
20. Ibid., p. 195.
21. Ibid., p. 197.
22. Ibid., p. 201.
23. R. L. Heilbroner, *An Inquiry into the Human Prospect*, W. W. Norton, New York 1975.
24. Ibid., p. 158.
25. Ibid., p. 165.

9. *Ideology and Beyond*

1. See especially Barry Commoner, *The Poverty of Power: Energy and the Economic Crisis*, Alfred A. Knopf, New York 1976.
2. John C. Bennett, *The Radical Imperative*, p. 156.
3. George Dalton, *Economic Systems and Society*, p. 197.
4. Joan Robinson, *Freedom and Necessity*, p. 124.

Index